MA'S BIT O' BRASS

"DEANE'S" SERIES OF PLAYS
General Editor : GEORGE W. BISHOP

MA'S BIT O' BRASS

A COMEDY IN THREE ACTS

By RONALD GOW

PRICE 5s. NET.

Cressrelles Publishing Co Ltd

10 Station Road Industrial Estate, Colwall,
Herefordshire WR14 6RN *Telephone:* 01684 540154

BOSTON, MASS., U.S.A. : WALTER H. BAKER COMPANY

PRINTED IN ENGLAND

All applications for performances by professional companies should be addressed to
The London Play Co. Ltd., 161 New Bond Street, W. 1.

Acting Fees for Performances Overseas

Apply—South Africa: Darter & Sons, Cape Town. Kenya: National Theatre, P.O. Box 452, Nairobi. Southern Rhodesia: Southern Rhodesian Drama Association, Private Box 167 H, Salisbury. Australia: Doreen Rayment, Flat 17, 229 Miller Street, North Sydney. New Zealand: John Bush Play Bureau, P.O. Box 273, Hawera. Canada and U.S.A.: Walter H. Baker Company, Boston.

THIS story of the Lovejoy family was originally designed in scenario form under the title of " Lancashire Luck," and made into a film by Paramount-British with George Carney, Muriel George and Wendy Hiller in the leading parts.

The play was first produced in July, 1938, by the Colwyn Bay Repertory Company with Sidney Dench and Clara Widdicombe as Mr. and Mrs. Lovejoy. It was later produced at the " Q " Theatre with George Carney and Marjorie Rhodes. A Welsh version entitled " Arian Sychion " has been published by Messrs. Gee of Denbigh.

CHARACTERS

(In order of Appearance)

BETTY LOVEJOY
A REPORTER
A PHOTOGRAPHER
GEORGE LOVEJOY
JOE LOVEJOY
AUNT NORAH
UNCLE ELIJAH
MRS. LOVEJOY
LADY MAYDEW
THE GROCER'S GIRL
GERALD
ROBINSON
SERGEANT BENNETT

SCENES

MA'S BIT O' BRASS

By Ronald Gow

ACT I.

SCENE I : *The kitchen of the house of* GEORGE LOVEJOY, *a foreman
carpenter in a North Country town. A window on the* R. *looks out on
the street, which is hidden from us by spotless muslin curtains. Late
afternoon sunshine streams in. The door in the back wall takes us into
a narrow passage, where the foot of the stairs is visible. By turning
to the left we would arrive at the front door. There is a kitchen fireplace on the* L. *A table is laid with tea for four, and a kettle is ready
on the hob. There is a couch under the window, and an easy chair by
the fire.*

The front door is unlocked and BETTY LOVEJOY *enters. She is a pretty
girl of about nineteen, neatly dressed, who is returning from her work.
She looks at the table as she takes off her hat and coat. She goes to the
door and calls " Hello, mother ! " She calls several times, but there
is no reply. She whistles. Then she looks in the oven. There is a
knock at the door. She goes to answer it. A man's voice asks for*
MRS. LOVEJOY.

BETTY (*outside*). I'm sorry. She's not in. What do you
want ?

MAN'S VOICE. I want to interview her.

BETTY. Well, she's not in. Who are you ?

MAN'S VOICE. All right, we'll come in and wait for her. It's
very important.

(*A* YOUNG MAN *appears, followed by* BETTY. *He has pushed his way
in. She follows, and another man, with a camera, follows her into the
room.*)

BETTY. Look here, you can't come in like that. Who are
you, anyway ? If it's insurance we don't want any, and if it's a
sewing machine we've got one.

YOUNG MAN. That's all right. Don't you worry. There's
my card. Special Correspondent *News Herald.*

BETTY. Do you mean you're a newspaper reporter?

YOUNG MAN. That's right. My colleague with camera.

(*The* COLLEAGUE *nods* " *How d'you do?* " *and seats himself by the fire.*)

BETTY. But—is there anything wrong?

YOUNG MAN. Bless you, no. (*Consulting a piece of paper.*) I suppose your mother *is* Mrs. George Lovejoy?

BETTY. Yes.

YOUNG MAN. And you say she's out?

BETTY. Yes.

YOUNG MAN. Gone to cash her cheque I expect. Well, you won't mind if we wait till she comes, will you?

(*He sits on the edge of the table, his feet on a chair. He lights a cigarette.*)

BETTY. Look here, what *is* the matter? What do you want with mother?

YOUNG MAN. I'll tell you. Your mother, Mrs. George Lovejoy, has won five hundred pounds in the United Football Pool.

BETTY. Five hundred pounds!

YOUNG MAN. That's right. The company's representative called here this morning. I was sent to get the full human story with photographs, and if I don't get it I get the sack. So you see, I've got to wait.

BETTY. Well, I suppose you'd better. Only father'll be in soon. . .

YOUNG MAN. He won't eat me, will he?

BETTY. He's a bit funny about—Football Pools. Says it's gambling. Mother does it on the quiet.

YOUNG MAN (*making a note*). Gosh! That's splendid. Anti-gambling husband in strange dilemma. Here, what about a picture of you while we're waiting?

BETTY. Of me?

YOUNG MAN. Yes. Got your camera, Jim? (*To* BETTY.) You sit here.

BETTY. But I haven't done anything.

(*She is pushed into a chair.*)

YOUNG MAN. No, but you're the heiress to the Lovejoy millions. Take this bit of paper and look at it. Imagine it's a cheque for five hundred pounds. Open your mouth a bit. That's right. But smile, smile. Show a bit of leg. (*He lifts her skirt.*) Now turn your eyes up—up—watch my hand—a life of luxury opens its vistas before you. (*He shouts.*) That's it. Hold it! Right, Jim.

(*There is a flash. They have not noticed that* Mr. Lovejoy, *a stolid man in a bowler hat, carrying a lunch-basket, has entered and is watching the process.*)

Lovejoy. Hey ! What the bloomin' heck's going on in here ?
Betty. Oh, dad ! I'm so glad you've come.

(*She runs to him.*)

Lovejoy. Here, what's all this ?
Betty. Mother's won five hundred pounds in a football pool.
Lovejoy. Nay ! There's some mistake. She's not that sort of woman.
Betty. This man's from the *News Herald*, and he wants to interview her.
Lovejoy. I'll interview him.

(*He pushes* Betty *aside and advances on the* Young Man, *who is sitting on the table again. The camera-man again sits by the fire.*)

Now, who the blazes do you think *you* are ?
Young Man (*offering a card*). Special Correspondent *News Herald*. My colleague, with camera. Are you Mr. Lovejoy ?
Lovejoy. Yes, I am.
Young Man. Take a seat, will you ?
Lovejoy. Well, I'll be danged ! Do you know this is my own house ?
Young Man. Of course. That's why I'm here.
Lovejoy (*turning to* Betty). Where's your ma ?
Betty. I don't know.
Young Man. Now, Mr. Lovejoy, perhaps you'll tell me what you mean to do with five hundred pounds.
Lovejoy. Here, what's all this about ? What do you chaps mean coming asking daft questions, and sitting on my table ? And who said my wife had won all that money ?
Young Man. My dear Mr. Lovejoy, your wife received a cheque from the United Football Pool Company this morning. I understand you don't approve of pools.
Lovejoy. No, I don't. Gambling, that's what it is. Ill-gotten money, and I don't hold with it. Fancy your mother doing that sort of thing.
Betty. But five hundred pounds !
Lovejoy. Aye . . . (*He scratches his head.*) It's a rare packet o' brass. (*To the* Young Man, *suddenly.*) Here—you don't think Government'll make pools illegal, do you ?
Young Man. Not before she's cashed the cheque, Mr. Lovejoy.
Lovejoy. Eh, Betty, I wish I knew where your ma had got to. Not like her to go off sudden like this.

YOUNG MAN. Have you any theories, Mr. Lovejoy ?

LOVEJOY. What do you mean—theories ?

YOUNG MAN. I mean—where do you think your wife would go to with a cheque for five hundred pounds in her pocket ?

LOVEJOY. What the flaming heck's it got to do with you ?

YOUNG MAN (*jotting in a notebook*). " ' What the flaming heck's it got to do with you ? ' said Mr. Lovejoy to our Special Correspondent."

LOVEJOY (*about to strike him*). Here you . . . get outside ! Get outside—do you hear me ?

YOUNG MAN (*to the photographer*). There you are, Bert. Get that !

(*The camera flashes and a picture is taken of* LOVEJOY *in a threatening attitude.*)

Portrait of happy husband receiving news of wife's good fortune.

LOVEJOY. Here—has he taken my photograph ?

YOUNG MAN. Yes, sir.

LOVEJOY. I'll photograph him !

(*He makes a dive at the photographer who darts to the door.* LOVEJOY *rushes at the* YOUNG MAN.)

Get out ! Get out, the pair of you ! By Gow, I've half a mind to kill you !

(*He seizes the* YOUNG MAN *and throws him into the passage and boots him out through the front door.* LOVEJOY *returns and removes his bowler hat.*)

Young fool ! Made me feel proper angry. Coming here with his daft questions.

BETTY. Yes, dad, but they *were* newspaper men. It's always better to be polite to the Press.

LOVEJOY. Press ! We've never had nowt to do with the Press in our family. We've always been respectable.

BETTY. They did put your name in the paper when you won the bowling championship.

LOVEJOY. Oh, well, that were different. What's for tea ?

BETTY. There's a hot-pot in the oven.

LOVEJOY. Who laid the table ?

BETTY. Mother must have done it before she went out. If we don't start eating the hot-pot it'll spoil.

LOVEJOY. Where's Joe ?

BETTY. He hasn't come yet. But he's always late. No good waiting for him. Come on, sit down.

(LOVEJOY *removes his coat and sits down in his shirt sleeves.* BETTY *puts the hot-pot in front of him. He is uneasy.*)

LOVEJOY. I wonder where your ma's got to?

BETTY. Perhaps she's gone up to see Aunt Norah.

LOVEJOY. Aunt Norah, my foot. She hasn't visited her for ten years.

BETTY. Then perhaps she's gone to the bank.

LOVEJOY. Bank closes at three o'clock.

BETTY. Well, get some hot-pot.

LOVEJOY. I'm not hungry, Betty.

BETTY. Not hungry. That's not like you.

LOVEJOY. And it's not like your ma to go off without warning. She tells me everything. It's taken my appetite away.

BETTY. I'm quite hungry, dad.

LOVEJOY. Oh, aye—of course. I'm sorry, lass.

(*He serves her with hot-pot.*)

BETTY. Better have some yourself.

LOVEJOY. I can't eat when I'm mithered.

(*She puts some on his plate.*)

BETTY. There you are. Just pick at that.

(*He eats absent-mindedly.*)

LOVEJOY. Money brings trouble, you mark my words.

BETTY. I wouldn't mind a bit of trouble so long as we had the money. Lot of things you could do with five hundred pounds.

LOVEJOY. We've always done very well without it. Not that we haven't been comfortable.

(*She hands him a cup of tea.*)

Though I did used to think sometimes when I were working in joiner's shop that a bit of capital'd come in handy like. I might have set up a timber yard on my own. Or I might have been a builder like Joe Ramsbottom and made a lot of money. But I've always been slow and sure, and your ma and me's been happy—and that's what counts in the end, lass. Happiness.

BETTY. Anyway, I can't see any harm in having the money. It may be gambling, but somebody's got to win.

LOVEJOY. If I was you I wouldn't be too sure of that money till it's safe in bank.

BETTY. That's a daft place to keep money. We could do with a new carpet, and I'd like a new party frock, and you and Joe want Sunday suits badly.

LOVEJOY. What's wrong with my old one?

BETTY. Well, it's an old one—that's all.

LOVEJOY. It's the suit I married your mother in, and I'm not going chopping and changing at my time of life.

BETTY. I know. You and ma could go on a cruise.

(*He splutters over his tea.*)

LOVEJOY. A cruise! What sort of a flibbertigibbet do you take me for?

BETTY. And perhaps you could take me and Joe along with you.

LOVEJOY. Here—I'm not discussing that money till I've seen the colour of it. As far as I'm concerned the money doesn't exist. In any case it's going to be invested. Railway shares, that's what we'll buy, and draw the divi.

BETTY. Shares go up and down. Much better spend it.

(*A knock on the door.*)

LOVEJOY. Now what's that? See who it is, Betty.

BETTY (*afraid*). Oh, I do hope it isn't anything . . .

(*Knock again.*)

LOVEJOY. If it's any more newspaper chaps I'm not at home.

(BETTY *goes.* LOVEJOY *takes a great deal more hot-pot.* BETTY *is heard talking with a man. She returns with two large boxes in brown paper from a shop.*)

BETTY. These have come for Mother. They're from Lewis's. She must have been shopping. (*She hands her father a bill.*) Seventeen and tenpence to pay.

LOVEJOY. What?

BETTY. They're C.O.D.

LOVEJOY. C.O.D.? What does that mean?

BETTY. It usually means Care of Dad. The man's waiting.

LOVEJOY. What the blooming heck does your mother think she's playing at? Seventeen shillings and tenpence. (*He takes out the money.*) There you are. Rent and beer money all at one go. I suppose she's been and bought a fur coat or summat.

(BETTY *goes with money.*)

Seventeen ruddy shillings and tenpence.

(*He takes up the parcel. Feels weight. Tears a bit of paper in an attempt to look inside. Drops it and sits down again.*)

(BETTY *returns.*)

BETTY. I wonder what's in them, Dad?

LOVEJOY. I don't know and I don't care.

BETTY. I hope she's not frittering that money away. (*She puts parcels behind couch. Hoots on horn.*)
LOVEJOY. Who's making all that noise?

(*There is a noisy rattle in the street, followed by repeated hoots on a horn.*)

Who's making all that noise?

(BETTY *rises and goes to the window.*)

BETTY. Sounds like a car.
LOVEJOY. See who it is.
BETTY (*at the window*). Well, I'm blowed!
LOVEJOY. What's to do?
BETTY. It's Joe. He's driving a car.
LOVEJOY. Whose car?
BETTY. I don't know. Here he comes.

(JOE, *a lad of seventeen, comes in.*)

JOE. I say, have you heard the news?
BETTY. Do you mean about mother?
JOE. Yes, isn't it grand! Five hundred.
BETTY. Aye, but where *is* your mother?
JOE. I don't know. She was in when I went out. What do you think of the car?
BETTY. Whose is it?
JOE. Mine—ours, I mean. (*He goes to the window.*) Isn't she a beauty?
BETTY. Where did you get it?
JOE. I've bought it.
LOVEJOY. Bought it?
JOE. Yes.
LOVEJOY (*going to the window*). Do you mean to tell me you've bought a motor car?
JOE. Well, I haven't paid for it yet. But the chap said I could pay in the morning.
LOVEJOY. What the blazes is wrong with the lad? Has he gone barmy?
JOE. It's a jolly good car.
BETTY. Where did you get the money, Joe?
JOE. I haven't got it yet. But I know Ma always wanted a car. She'll pay all right. And it's licensed for another two months—*and* insured.
LOVEJOY. You young fool! How much have you gone and paid for that?
JOE. Only two pounds ten. He wanted two pounds twelve and six, but I beat him down.

LOVEJOY. Well, you can blooming well take it back where you got it.

JOE. But Ma wants a car, and now she's won all that money. . . .

LOVEJOY. Dammit ! We've not seen your mother or the money yet ! And see here, where's your driving licence ?

JOE (*producing it*). Here. They got it for me when I worked at garage. But it's—three months out of date.

LOVEJOY. You mean it's expired ?

JOE. Mother'll let me have five bob for a new one.

LOVEJOY. Listen to him. Talks like a blasted millionaire. Do you mean you're breaking the law ?

JOE. Well, in a sort of way . . .

LOVEJOY. I won't have you breaking the law, do you hear ? It's the principle of the thing I care about. Besides, you might get copped.

JOE. Any tea left, Betty ?

(BETTY *has put some hot-pot on a plate.*)

BETTY. Here you are. It's cold, but you must be used to that.

(JOE *sits down and eats.*)

LOVEJOY. And where do you think you're going to keep it ? Supposing we did buy it. (*Fiercely.*) Only supposing, mind.

JOE. Mr. Simmonds says I can keep it in his shed for the time being.

LOVEJOY. For the time being ! And what happens after that ?

BETTY. Well, from the look of it, it'll fall to pieces long before then.

LOVEJOY. Yes, he's been done. Two pounds ten !

JOE. Well, it *goes*, anyway.

LOVEJOY (*meaningly*). Yes, it'll *go* all right. Back to where it came from.

(MR. LOVEJOY *stands at the fire filling his pipe.* BETTY *moves some of the dirty pots.*)

You see, Betty, money brings trouble. Where's the matches ?

BETTY. Up there.

(*He takes a box from the mantel-shelf and lights his pipe.*)

LOVEJOY. I'm going round to see Jim Ashworth. Happen he knows summat about your mother.

(*He gets his cap from behind door.*)

And think on, lad. When I get back I don't want to see no more of yon blasted contraption outside. You've got to take it away.

JOE. I can't.

LOVEJOY. Why can't you?

JOE. I've no licence, and I can't go breaking the law.

LOVEJOY (*furious*). You young . . .

BETTY (*sweetly*). Dad . . .

LOVEJOY. What is it?

BETTY. Just a minute.

(*She gives him his cap from behind the door. In his anger he has put on her red beret.*)

LOVEJOY. Aach!

(*He goes out.*)

BETTY. Poor old dad! You know, I think he really likes that car all the time.

(*She comes over to the table and kneels on a chair speaking to* JOE *and facing the window.*)

JOE. Do you think he does?

BETTY. Of course. But he's a bit frightened it isn't true about the money.

JOE. It's true enough.

BETTY. Still, you are a bit of a one doing a thing like that.

JOE. Well, if I didn't do it nobody would. They'd have talked and talked . . .

BETTY (*looking at the window*). I say, just look there.

JOE. What is it?

BETTY. Dad's looking at the car.

(*She runs to the window and peeps.*)

He's polishing the shiny part with his handkerchief.

JOE (*running to window*). Gosh! He's fallen for it. I thought he would. It's a marvellous bus—only nine years old—but it's a four-seater and it'd take us anywhere.

(*They turn away from the window.*)

BETTY. It's hard to believe, isn't it?

JOE. By gum, it is!

BETTY. Wealth beyond the dreams of avarice . . .

JOE. Now, wait a minute. Don't go running away with the idea you can do what you like with this money.

BETTY. Well, no, it *is* mother's money, isn't it?

JOE. Yes, but of course in a way I won it for her.

(*He sits at the table.* BETTY *pours out his tea.*)

B

BETTY. You did?

JOE. I gave her professional advice on football teams.

BETTY. Well, I like that. You may have given her advice but it was always wrong.

JOE. It wasn't.

(*He takes a bit of paper from his pocket and bites a piece of cake.*)

What mother wants is a financial adviser.

BETTY. What?

JOE. A financial adviser. I've got it all worked out.

BETTY. *You* have?

JOE (*chewing*). You see, we're in the capitalist class now.

BETTY. Well, don't talk with your mouth full.

JOE (*taking up his cup*): We've got to change all our ideas.

BETTY. Yes, we have. Don't drink till you've emptied your mouth.

JOE (*ignoring her*). Shut up. I've been figuring things out.

BETTY. What things?

JOE. How we're going to spend the money.

BETTY. Oh, have you?

JOE. This money's capital and we've got to put it in a productive enterprise. Now, if ma would set me up in a garage like I've always wanted . . .

BETTY. I don't call you a productive enterprise.

JOE. No, but if I had a garage I would be . . .

(MR. LOVEJOY *appears. He is carrying an evening paper.*)

LOVEJOY. It's true! It's in the paper!

JOE. Didn't I tell you?

(BETTY *takes the paper.*)

BETTY. Here, let me look.

LOVEJOY. Everybody's stopping me on t'street, and congratulating me. (*He chuckles.*) By gum! It's a do!

(BETTY *mixes the paper.* JOE *tries to look too.*)

Here, give it me. You've got it all mixed up.

(*He takes the paper.*)

Look, there you are. " Lancashire Woman's Luck in Penny Pool."

JOE (*reading over his shoulder*). " . . . the wife of an ordinary working man."

LOVEJOY. What's that? Where does it say that?

JOE. There.

LOVEJOY. But I'm not an ordinary working man. I'm a skilled carpenter.

BETTY. Never mind. It's true about the money.

LOVEJOY. Aye, that's all very well, but it doesn't explain where your ma's gone to. Nobody's seen or heard of her. I tell you, I'm fair mithered.

(*The sound of a car outside.*)

BETTY. Here's somebody in a car now.

JOE. Heck ! I hope she hasn't gone and bought another.

(*He bounds to the door.*)

BETTY. It's a taxi. It's mother. No, it isn't.

LOVEJOY. Go on, your mother wouldn't be seen dead in a taxi.

BETTY. It's Aunt Norah, and Uncle Elijah. . . .

LOVEJOY. What the heck's brought them here ?

BETTY. They're all dressed up. Quick, get these pots off.

(*She carries pots to the sideboard.*)

LOVEJOY. Now what does that Nosey Parker want coming now ?

(JOE *appears, leading* AUNT NORAH, *an acid-looking woman, and her husband* ELIJAH, *a much-trodden worm.*)

JOE (*as he enters*). It's Aunt Norah and Uncle Elijah.

(NORAH *goes straight to* LOVEJOY *and flings her arms round his neck.*)

NORAH. Oh, George, George ! What wonderful news !

LOVEJOY (*tea-pot in hand*). Now then. That'll do, that'll do. What's brought you here ?

NORAH. It's true, isn't it ?

LOVEJOY. Aye, but what are you all dressed up for ? Have you been to a funeral, or summat ?

NORAH. Dear Betty ! (*She kisses her.*) How are you ? It is true, isn't it ? I mean about your mother winning all that money ?

BETTY. Yes. It's true.

NORAH. You don't look very happy about it, any of you.

LOVEJOY. We don't mind the money, but we weren't expecting relations.

NORAH. Don't be a tease, George. Where's Mary ? We've come to congratulate her.

ELIJAH. That's right. Congratulate her.

NORAH. We thought it was about time we paid you a visit, anyway.

LOVEJOY. First time you've visited us in ten years. Bit late, aren't you?

NORAH. Don't be outspoken, George. It doesn't do. Specially in front of the children. There's always a time to let bygones be bygones, don't you think? And if there's going to be any merry-making over Mary's good fortune—well, the whole family should join in, I say.

ELIJAH. That's right.

LOVEJOY. Well, you've come to the wrong shop for merry-making. The missus is out, and till she comes home I've nowt to tell you.

NORAH. Out, is she? Where do you think she's gone?

LOVEJOY. Happen she's got some private business of her own.

NORAH. She's not gone out with all that money in her pocket?

LOVEJOY. How do I know?

NORAH. You mean you don't know where she's gone?

BETTY. Mother may have business with her lawyer.

NORAH. Nay, not at this time of day. (*Intensely.*) George!

LOVEJOY. Well?

NORAH. You don't think she's *left* you, do you?

LOVEJOY. Don't be a fool, Norah! How the hell do I know where she's gone to?

NORAH. Hush, George! Not before the children.

LOVEJOY. Oh, damn the children!

ELIJAH. Now, come, come . . .

LOVEJOY. You shut up!

BETTY. Aunt Norah, would you like a cup of tea?

NORAH. No, thank you, I've been insulted.

(*She sits down.*)

NORAH. I think on an occasion like this George might be a little more pleasant spoken.

BETTY. Father's very worried. You see, we really don't know where mother is. I'll put the kettle on.

(BETTY *does so.*)

NORAH. Well, I think it's very serious. I ought to have been told. After all, she is my sister.

ELIJAH. Hadn't we better tell the police?

LOVEJOY. What for?

ELIJAH. Happen they'll drag canal.

BETTY. Oh, Uncle . . .

LOVEJOY. Don't talk soft.

NORAH. Whose car was that I saw outside?

LOVEJOY. That? (*He catches* JOE's *eye and coughs.*) We thought of buying it. (*At* JOE.) Only thought of it, mind you.

NORAH. A car! Won't that be nice—for picnics and things?

LOVEJOY. No. It only holds four.

NORAH. Fancy—a motor car! Oh, she's a deep 'un, is Mary.

LOVEJOY. I don't see why we shouldn't have a car if we want.

JOE (*chiming in*). Neither do I.

LOVEJOY. You shut up!

(*A car draws up outside.*)

NORAH. What's that?

JOE. It's a car.

ELIJAH. I expect it's a nambulance.

BETTY. It is mother this time. And she's come in a car.

NORAH. It's a very big car, too.

JOE. Gosh! Perhaps she *has* bought one!

(*He darts out.* AUNT NORAH *and* ELIJAH *go to the window.* LOVE-JOY *remains in front of the fire.* JOE *enters first.*)

JOE. It's mother all right.

(MRS. LOVEJOY *enters. She is a stout, cheerful little Lancashire woman, with a rough edge to her tongue when wanted. She has her best clothes on.* BETTY *moves up to greet her, but everyone hangs back waiting for an announcement.*)

LOVEJOY. So you've come at last.

MRS. LOVEJOY (*taking off her hat*). Did you all get your teas? Hello, Betty dear. Well, Norah, this is a surprise. What brought you here? And Elijah, too. Well, I don't know.

NORAH. We wanted to be the first to congratulate you.

ELIJAH. It is true, isn't it? About the money?

MRS. LOVEJOY. It's true enough.

BETTY (*hugging her*). Oh, you darling!

JOE. I say, ma, can you let me have a few pounds?

NORAH. Listen to Joe!

LOVEJOY (*to* JOE). You shut your trap, and let your mother rest.

MRS. LOVEJOY (*sitting by the table*). Eee, I'm that tired. And me feet is twice their size.

(*She is taking off her shoes.* NORAH, *to her surprise, kneels and helps her.*)

NORAH. We was thinking that happen our combined families might have a day at Blackpool or somewhere—sort of celebration like.

Mrs. Lovejoy (*coldly*). Oh? Who was thinking that?

Norah. Me and Elijah.

Mrs. Lovejoy. And who's going to pay?

Norah. We thought it'd be a nice idea if you took us like.

Elijah. That's right.

Lovejoy. Oh! Would it? Well, just you listen to me, Norah Higson, that money's going to be invested.

Betty. Not all of it. Mother and father are going on a cruise, and I shouldn't wonder if they took me and Joe along with them.

Joe. And, look here, ma, didn't you say you always wanted a car? Well, I've bought one.

Mrs. Lovejoy. Well, I don't know. You've all made up your minds pretty quick what I'm going to do with my own money.

Norah. We was only being helpful.

Lovejoy. You're sure you've really got the money?

Mrs. Lovejoy. Got it? *I've spent it.*

(*General consternation.*)

Lovejoy. ⎰ Spent it?
Joe.   ⎱ Oh, ma!
Norah.   ⎰ Mary, you haven't!

Mrs. Lovejoy. I have. Most of it, anyway. And a good job too, I'm thinking.

Lovejoy. You don't mean to tell me you've gone and spent five hundred pounds?

Mrs. Lovejoy. There's not much left.

Lovejoy. You must have gone mad.

Norah (*rising*). Well, I don't think we're welcome here, somehow, Elijah, we'd better be going.

Elijah. That's right.

Mrs. Lovejoy. Yes, Norah, I think you had.

(*It is growing darker outside.*)

Norah. And let me give you a piece of advice, Mary. You always were a soft one. Anybody as wants can impose on you. I don't know what you've done with your money, but I do know the claims of your own flesh and blood should come first.

Mrs. Lovejoy. A soft one, am I? Well, you aren't the one that's going to impose on me. Good night to you.

Norah. Oh very well. Good night.

(*She goes to the door with* Elijah.)

Money goes to some folks' heads.

(*She turns for a parting shot.*)

You was a kind-hearted sister once, but now the iron has entered into your soul.

Mrs. Lovejoy. Aye, maybe so, but brass stays in me pocket.

(Norah *goes, with dignity.* Lovejoy *closes the door.* Betty *gives her mother a cup of tea.*)

Lovejoy (*shutting door*). There. Norah's the sort that looks a lot better going than coming.

Mrs. Lovejoy. Thank you, Betty. That's just what I want.

(Joe *has got a chair for her feet.*)

Joe. Now put your feet up on this.

Mrs. Lovejoy. Thank you, Joe.

Lovejoy. Have you had owt to eat?

Mrs. Lovejoy. Aye, I'm all right, thanks. This'll do me fine.

Joe. I say, ma, didn't you always say you wanted a car?

Mrs. Lovejoy (*smiling*). Is that it outside?

Joe. Yes. It's twelve horse-power, and it's got coil ignition and four-wheel brakes. Suit us fine.

Mrs. Lovejoy. Give me my purse off the table.

Joe. It cost two ten, and I'll want another pound for gadgets and things.

Mrs. Lovejoy. Here you are.

Lovejoy. Here, half a minute.

Mrs. Lovejoy (*giving* Joe *some money*). It's my money, George, and the lad knows what he's doing.

Lovejoy. Well, I'm jiggered!

Joe. Oh, thanks, ma.

Lovejoy. But we can't afford a motor car.

Mrs. Lovejoy. A car's just what we want in the country.

Lovejoy. In the country.

Mrs. Lovejoy. Yes, we're going to live in a cottage in the country.

Lovejoy. A cottage in the country!

Mrs. Lovejoy. That's what I said. I've got a little plan.

Lovejoy. Gosh! She *has* gone daft.

(*He sits down suddenly.*)

Betty (*humouring her*). Which cottage do you mean, ma?

Mrs. Lovejoy. I bought one this afternoon. Right in the country it is. On the road to Chester. That's where I've been, and I've just come back in young baronet's car.

Betty. A baronet's car?

Mrs. Lovejoy. Of course, baronet wasn't driving himself, but chauffeur was. I bought the cottage off his agent.

LOVEJOY (*coming over to her*). Did you say you'd bought a cottage ?

MRS. LOVEJOY. Well, why not ?

LOVEJOY. Aye, but *why* ?

MRS. LOVEJOY. Because I'm sick of the town and everything in it. That's why. Isn't it time I had a bit of my own way ? We're going to strike out afresh.

JOE. That's right. Pioneers !

LOVEJOY. But what about my job ? I'm a skilled carpenter. My job's in the town.

MRS. LOVEJOY. *I'll* give you a job in the country.

LOVEJOY. You'll give *me* a job ?

MRS. LOVEJOY. Haven't you given me a job all my life at the kitchen sink ? Well, now I'll give *you* a job. There's plenty to do on a farm.

BETTY (*worried*). Do you mean a farm with cows and things ?

MRS. LOVEJOY. We'll have that some day. First of all we're going to open a tea garden. You'll run that, Betty. And there's room to build a garage for our Joe.

JOE. Hooray ! Where is it ?

MRS. LOVEJOY. It's out at Wishton where all the cyclists and hikers go.

BETTY. Doesn't it sound grand ?

LOVEJOY (*sinking weakly into his chair*). Whatever's come over you, ma ? I've never seen you like this before.

MRS. LOVEJOY. It's wonderful the confidence a bit of brass gives you. And I've got quite a bit left for working expenses.

JOE (*putting it on*). Well, mother, I think I'll garage the car. Are you coming to help me, Betty ?

BETTY. Right, I'll come.

(*She goes to her father on the way to the door and kisses the top of his head.*)

It's all right, dad. Don't look so worried. We'll manage.

LOVEJOY. I were just wondering if I'd wake up and find I'd been dreaming.

MRS. LOVEJOY (*rising*). No, lad, you weren't snoring loud enough for that.

BETTY (*her arm round his neck*). It'll be grand ! We'll be striking out into the west like settlers in covered wagons. Buck up, dad !

(*She runs out after* JOE. *The car starts up and goes.* LOVEJOY *sits staring moodily before him.* MRS. LOVEJOY *goes about her kitchen business, keeping her eye on him.*)

LOVEJOY (*suddenly*). It's not April First, is it ?

Mrs. Lovejoy. No, George, owd lad, I'm not joking. You know well enough I didn't do a thing like that without thinking.

Lovejoy. But it's so sudden.

Mrs. Lovejoy. There wasn't much future for us in the town, George. Joe out of a job, and Betty in a shop. You haven't been looking too clever yourself lately, either. Well, we'll get fresh air where we're going if we get nowt else.

(*She puts the tea-things on a tray.*)

How much notice do we have to give to leave this house?

Lovejoy. A week, if the rent's paid.

Mrs. Lovejoy. Then we move into Wimple Cottage a week to-morrow.

(*She goes to the scullery door with tray.*)

Lovejoy. Here, hold on, hold on! I haven't been consulted, you know.

Mrs. Lovejoy (*going*). No time for consultations, George.

Lovejoy (*shouting after her*). I think you might have asked my opinion first. Do you want to make me look a fool?

Mrs. Lovejoy (*popping her head in again*). You'll look a darned sight worse fool if you stop on here in an empty house, George.

(*His jaw drops.*)

CURTAIN.

Note.—It is essential that the interval between these scenes be kept as short as possible. Two minutes should be ample time in which to remove furniture, ornaments, curtains, pictures, etc., particularly if all these things have been arranged for a quick change.

Scene 2. *The room is cleared of its furniture, with the exception of the table and a chair. Boxes and bundles lie about the room. A piece of old sackcloth screens the lower part of the window. A barrel-organ is playing down the street.*

Lovejoy *is sitting in the same position, and in the same chair, as at the Curtain of the last scene. He looks miserable. The* Removal Men *enter. They pull away the table on which his elbow is leaning and carry it out.*

Betty *enters. She is dressed for setting out.*

Betty. I say, Dad, you can't sit there!

(*She busily picks things up.*)

Lovejoy. Why can't I sit here?

BETTY. Because the lorry's just going, and there's all these things to go in Joe's motor car.

LOVEJOY. Gah ! I'm fair sick to death of the whole business.

BETTY. Now, Dad ! Don't be narky. Why don't you shape a bit better ?

LOVEJOY. Shape ? Your mother's just told me to keep out of the road.

BETTY. Do be cheerful, Dad.

LOVEJOY. Cheerful ! How do you expect a man to be cheerful when his own wife's leading him down the road to ruin ?

BETTY (*taking bundle to the door*). Go on. It won't be so bad. We'll have some fun, anyway.

LOVEJOY. Fun. That's all your generation thinks about.

(*A* REMOVAL MAN *enters.*)

Too much chopping and changing in the world to-day. What we want is more safety first . . .

(*The* MAN *is tapping his shoulder and indicating that he wants the chair.*)

What ? (*He rises.*) Yes, take it ! Take the whole blooming lot. Take me as well if you like. I'm only a chattel.

(*The* MAN *goes out. A* NEIGHBOUR *looks in at the window.*)

NEIGHBOUR. Hello, Mr. Lovejoy ! Are you flitting ?

LOVEJOY (*to* BETTY). Are we flitting ? (*To* NEIGHBOUR.) No, you fool, we're nobbut taking things out for an airing !

BETTY. I think people are awful. There's quite a crowd watching outside.

(JOE *runs in.*)

JOE. Hey ! He says he hopes that's the lot because there's no more room on the lorry.

BETTY. Take that to him. Quick !

(*She gives* JOE *the bundle.*)

JOE. But he's just starting.

BETTY. Run after him. Hurry !

(JOE *runs.* MRS. LOVEJOY *comes downstairs with various things, including a cardboard box of odds and ends.*)

MRS. LOVEJOY. Well, I think that's about all.

BETTY. We'll have to put the rest in the car. The lorry's going.

Mrs. Lovejoy.   Going ?   Drat it, I meant to put your father on the lorry.

Lovejoy (*indignant*).   You meant to put . . .

Mrs. Lovejoy.   Just to keep an eye on things, George.   Here, take that stuff and put it in Joe's car.

Lovejoy.   What's all this rubbish ?   You're not taking these ?

Mrs. Lovejoy.   Now don't start again.   There's been quite enough arguments.   Go on, out of my road !

(*She flourishes a brush.   He goes quickly.   BETTY picks up a case of stuffed birds.*)

Betty.   Not these, Mother.   Nobody has stuffed birds nowadays.

Mrs. Lovejoy.   I'm not so set on 'em myself, but your father's very proud of them.

Betty (*going to scullery*).   Oh, is he ?

Mrs. Lovejoy.   What are you going to do ?

Betty.   These are going to be lost in transit.   I'm putting them in the dust-bin.

(*She is going out with them when her father comes in.   He looks suspicious.*)

Lovejoy.   Hey, Betty !   Where are you taking those ?   Come here.

(*He takes them from her.*)

Mrs. Lovejoy.   We was thinking you wouldn't want these any more.

Lovejoy.   But them's my stuffed birds.

Betty.   They're very old-fashioned, Dad.

Lovejoy.   Are they ?   So am I old-fashioned.   And proud of it.   Do you know these belonged to my mother?

(*He goes out with the birds.*)

Mrs. Lovejoy.   Won't let me throw anything away.   He's always been like that.

Betty.   I suppose we've got to humour him.   I'm taking this lot.

Mrs. Lovejoy (*at window*).   Hey, George !   Not there.   That's where I'm going to sit.

(BETTY *goes out with a load.   MRS. LOVEJOY gathers things up.   JOE enters followed by the* REPORTER.)

Joe.   I say, Mother—here's that newspaper reporter.

Mrs. Lovejoy.   Hello, what do you want ?

Reporter. Good morning, Mrs. Lovejoy. I see I'm only just in time. My paper would like a few words from you.

(Joe *picks up something and goes out.*)

Mrs. Lovejoy. Nay, lad, I've no time for you this morning.
Reporter. I understand you're moving into the country.
Mrs. Lovejoy (*picking up a bundle*). That's right. Out of my road.
Reporter (*persistent*). Going to open a tea-garden, I hear.

(Lovejoy *appears.*)

Mrs. Lovejoy. Look here, lad, I'm busy. You'd best speak to my husband. He'll tell you all about it. It's his idea really.
Lovejoy. My what? What are you doing here? Didn't I tell you I didn't want to see your ugly mug again?
Mrs. Lovejoy. All right, George. He's only earning his living same as anybody else.

(*She goes.*)

Reporter. I congratulate you, Mr. Lovejoy, on your courage and your initiative.
Lovejoy. Congratulate *me?*
Reporter. I hear you're going to open a tea-garden?
Lovejoy. Here, what's the idea?
Reporter. I'd like you to give a little message to our readers.
Lovejoy. What, me?
Reporter. Yes, of course. We're making quite a feature of it. I'd like a photograph as well.
Lovejoy (*attracted*). You want me to make a statement like?
Reporter. Exactly. Spirit of adventure still flourishing, and all that sort of thing. I suppose the tea-garden *was* your idea?
Lovejoy (*his eye on the door*). Er—oh, yes. Just a minute. (*He looks out.*) You tell 'em this. That I hope to prove—by my action to-day—that the—er—spirit of er . . .
Reporter. Spirit of adventure.
Lovejoy. That's it. The spirit of adventure is still flourishing in Lancashire. We are striking into the West—like—er—settlers in covered wagons. Got that? What this country needs is change. Too much safety first nowadays. How's that?
Reporter. Splendid. I'll fill it out. (*Going*) Now I'd just like another word with your wife.
Lovejoy. And remember—when you put that in the paper—I'm a skilled carpenter—not an ordinary working man.

REPORTER. Right you are.

(*He goes.* JOE *looks in.*)

JOE. I say, Dad, I wish you'd come and help me start the car. It won't go.

LOVEJOY. All right. I'm coming.

(*He goes.* MRS. LOVEJOY *comes in with the dust-bin from the scullery. She looks round the room. The street-organ plays. She sits down on the dust-bin and weeps.* LOVEJOY *calls and enters.*)

LOVEJOY. Hey, Mother ! Oh, there you are. We've started the car, and Joe says we've got to get going before it stops. Here—what's to do ? What's the matter, missus ?

(*He puts his arm round her.*)

What are you crying for ?

MRS. LOVEJOY. It's nowt.

(*She borrows his handkerchief.*)

LOVEJOY. Must be tired. Here, I haven't said anything harsh to you, have I ?

MRS. LOVEJOY. It's—leaving the old home.

LOVEJOY. Leaving the old home ! Well, I'm blowed ! And whose fault is that, I'd like to know ?

MRS. LOVEJOY. Don't be angry with me.

LOVEJOY. Nay, I'm not angry. (*He scratches his head.*) But I'm fair puzzled.

MRS. LOVEJOY. Do you think it's all for the best ?

LOVEJOY. It'd better be, for I'm noan turning back now.

MRS. LOVEJOY. Twenty-five years. It's a long time to have lived here, and then leave sudden like this.

LOVEJOY. Nay, don't take on about that.

MRS. LOVEJOY (*a smile*). Do you remember first time we came here, after our honeymoon ?

LOVEJOY. Honeymoon ? Well, you can call it that if you like. Day at Blackpool I call it.

MRS. LOVEJOY. You remember how tired we were—and we sat in a chair by the fire, and I went to sleep on your knee ?

LOVEJOY. Aye, I remember. It still gives me cramp in my leg when I think of it.

MRS. LOVEJOY. You were too polite to waken me in those days, George.

LOVEJOY (*laughing*). Aye. We've had some times here, we have and all. Do you remember the night when . . . ?

(*Insistent hooting and shouting from outside.*)

LOVEJOY. Well, come on, Joe's getting impatient.

MRS. LOVEJOY (*wiping her eyes*). Aye, we've got to go now. Have you got front door key?

LOVEJOY. I've got it.

MRS. LOVEJOY. I think that's everything. (*Calling.*) All right, we're coming.

(*She goes to the door, and turns. She smiles at* LOVEJOY *and suddenly kisses him. He looks surprised.*)

LOVEJOY. By gum, ma!

He hurries after her. More shouts and cheers. LOVEJOY *runs back, picks up the kettle, and runs out with it.*)

CURTAIN.

ACT II.

Scene 1. *The kitchen at Wimple Cottage. Low beams and plaster walls. A door and a long low window in the back wall. A hedge hides the garden from us, which is reached by turning right at the door. By turning left we reach the gate. On the* L. *a large fireplace. Above the fireplace a staircase. There is a sink in the top* R. *hand corner and over it a smaller window. The furniture is mainly that of Act I. A long table below the window is covered with cups, saucers, plates, trays and food. It is Saturday morning.* Mrs. Lovejoy *takes some loaves from the oven and carries them to the table.* Betty *sits working out accounts at the* C. *table.* Mrs. Lovejoy *goes back to the fire to make some tea. There is a sound of hammering outside.*

Betty. Well, we've not done badly. That's all profit. And another thing, we must start a bank account. You can't have all that money about the house.

Mrs. Lovejoy. I don't like a bank knowing how much money I've got.

Betty. Last Saturday was the best day we've had. And I expect we'll do twice as well to-day.

(Mrs. Lovejoy *goes to the door and calls.*)

Mrs. Lovejoy. Ge-orge ! Jo-oe ! Cup of tea !

(*There is a faint reply.* Betty *gets tea-cups.*)

Betty. They ought to finish that garage to-day, then Joe can start earning. And I've been thinking, ma, if we can use that room over the barn we'll have five bedrooms for letting to visitors.

Mrs. Lovejoy. Now, steady on, lass. Let's make sure of what we've got first. Though we haven't done badly in three weeks. There's your tea.

(Lovejoy *enters. He is in shirt-sleeves, but he still wears his bowler.*)

Cup of tea, George ?

Lovejoy. Aye, I'm fair parched.

Mrs. Lovejoy. Where's Joe ?

Lovejoy. He's coming. He's painting that new sign-board. I say, Betty, how many " m's " in " accommodation " ?

Betty. Two, of course.

LOVEJOY. Nay, I thought there was only one. Well, you're a scholar. You ought to know. By gum! There seems to be plenty of brass in the kitty.

BETTY. We've done very well. Here's a statement of accounts for last Saturday. (*She reads.*) " Gross takings on sale of teas— Three pounds, fourteen shillings and sixpence. Expenses—cost of teas, broken pottery, etc. . . ."

LOVEJOY. Here, never mind broken pottery. Tell us what we've made.

BETTY. The net profit's two pounds, two shillings and fourpence halfpenny.

MRS. LOVEJOY. I call that champion.

LOVEJOY. Aye, and I reckon if weather holds good there'll be twice as much to-day. We've got a regular gold mine here. I always said we'd do well.

BETTY (*writing*). How many loaves is that, mother?

MRS. LOVEJOY. That's two dozen. We aren't going to run short like we did last Saturday, and all those people waiting.

BETTY. And I ordered double quantity of cream from Mrs. Brownlow. Do you think that'll be enough?

MRS. LOVEJOY. Make it three quarts. We're going to get a name for good helpings. That'll bring 'em again.

LOVEJOY. I've been thinking, ma, we ought to keep a cow.

MRS. LOVEJOY. What do you want with a cow?

LOVEJOY. I don't know. I've always had a fancy for cows.

MRS. LOVEJOY. Oh, have you!

BETTY. And I thought it'd be a good idea if we could sell honey.

(JOE *enters.*)

JOE. Honey? Is our Betty going to keep a bee?

MRS. LOVEJOY (*to* JOE). Here's some tea. Why can't you come when you're called?

BETTY. Have you painted that notice?

JOE. Not finished it yet. I say, Betty, how many " m's " in " accommodation "?

LOVEJOY (*quickly*). Two, of course.

JOE. Two? But you said. . . .

LOVEJOY. I said there was *two*.

MRS. LOVEJOY. Time that notice was up. What have you put on it, Joe?

JOE. I've put " Teas " in big letters. And underneath it " Plain or Knife and Fork." And then " Accommodation for Cyclists."

MRS. LOVEJOY. You and your dad put it up right away. There's nowt like publicity.

LOVEJOY. Garage is nigh on ready. We've only to hang doors.

JOE. That corner down the road's a good place for accidents. I'm hoping it'll bring some business. I could do with a good repair job. Selling petrol isn't much cop without a pump, and so far I've only had two punctures and the Vicar.

MRS. LOVEJOY. What did Vicar want?

JOE. Petrol for his lighter. All he gave me was a welcome to church on Sunday morning.

MRS. LOVEJOY. Well, you two, get on with your work. I've got a lot to do and you're in the way here.

(LOVEJOY *rises.*)

LOVEJOY. Come on, Joe. We'd best be going.

(JOE *finishes his tea.*)

JOE. Right. (*To* BETTY.) How many " m's " did you say there were in " accommodation " ?

BETTY. Two. Here you are.

(*She writes it down.*)

JOE. It's a rum word. I very near put a " c " instead of a " k." (*He looks at the piece of paper.*) Oh, that's how you spell it, is it? You know, I think we'll put " Bed and Breakfast " instead. It's safer.

BETTY (*laughing*). I think you'd better.

(*He follows his father outside.*)

Wonderful how dad's settled down.

MRS. LOVEJOY. Of course, I knew he would all the time. Taken to the country like a duck to the water, bless his old heart. (*She happens to look through the window.*) George! Don't sit there smoking and wearing out the seat of your pants. Get that notice put up, you lazy old scoundrel. (*To* BETTY.) Bless him!

BETTY. It's true what they say about Lancashire folk, mother.

MRS. LOVEJOY. What's that?

BETTY. Hard tongue and soft heart.

MRS. LOVEJOY. Aye, better'n a hard heart and a soft tongue, any day. Come on, now, get them pots washed up.

(BETTY *washes up at the sink in the corner.* MRS. LOVEJOY *busies herself with pans and cooking.*)

BETTY. The Northern Hiking Club are coming out to Wishton Hill before the end of the month. That'll mean hundreds.

c

Mrs. Lovejoy. We'll be busy at that rate.

Betty. Last Bank Holiday they say there were more than a thousand people came to Wishton. Wonder to me there hasn't been a tea place here before.

Mrs. Lovejoy. The estate wouldn't allow it, that's why. I only got this cottage because they're hard up and it wasn't much use to them.

Betty. Some day I don't see why we shouldn't run a regular hotel here.

Mrs. Lovejoy. Bless you! Well, *you've* taken to the country all right, lass.

(Joe *calls outside and enters.*)

Joe. I say, mother!

Mrs. Lovejoy. What is it, Joe?

Joe. We've just put that notice up and there's a lady come along and says we've got to take it down.

Betty. Take it down?

Joe. Yes.

Mrs. Lovejoy. Rubbish! What's her name?

Joe. I don't know. Seems to think she's bought the blooming earth.

Mrs. Lovejoy. I'll talk to her.

Betty (*at the window*). She's coming in.

(Lovejoy *passes the window with a lady. He enters.*)

Lovejoy. Here, ma. I don't know what this old girl's talking about. (*He speaks outside.*) Hey! You'd better come in and see the missus.

(*He beckons and* Lady Maydew *enters. She is a strong, deep-chested woman, in the traditional " lady of the manor " style.*)

Lady Maydew (*to* Mrs. Lovejoy). Are you the proprietor of this—this venture?

Mrs. Lovejoy. I own this cottage, if that's what you mean.

Lady Maydew. I'm not so sure of that. However, are you responsible for that notice?

Mrs. Lovejoy. It's our notice. What's the matter? Is it spelt wrong?

Lady Maydew. I am Lady Maydew.

Mrs. Lovejoy. Pleased to meet you. Will you sit down?

Lady Maydew. No, thank you.

Mrs. Lovejoy. Well, you know best.

Lady Maydew. The villagers call me " your ladyship."

Mrs. Lovejoy. That's very nice of them, I'm sure. My name's

Mrs. Lovejoy. That's my husband. This is our Betty and this is our Joe.

Lady Maydew. Indeed ? You bought this cottage from my agent while I was away on holiday.

Mrs. Lovejoy. Did I ? I hope you had a nice time.

Lady Maydew. Unfortunately my son doesn't take much interest in the estate, or he would have stopped the sale. It would never have happened if *I* had been at home.

Mrs. Lovejoy. Oh ?

Lovejoy. Here, isn't anybody going to sit down ?

Lady Maydew. I prefer to stand.

Lovejoy. Well, I don't. Not when *women* are talking.

(*He sits by the fire and smokes his pipe.*)

Mrs. Lovejoy. Well, Lady Maydew, we're busy. Perhaps you'll be good enough to tell us what you've come for ?

Lady Maydew. First of all, that notice. I am the local president of the Society for the Preservation of Merrie England, and part of my work is the prevention of the destruction of rural amenities.

Mrs. Lovejoy. Are you criticising that notice? Because our Joe did it.

Lady Maydew. I *am* criticising that notice. You must take it down at once.

Mrs. Lovejoy. Why ?

Lady Maydew. Because it's defacing the beauty of the countryside.

Mrs. Lovejoy. And who says so ?

Lady Maydew. I do.

Mrs. Lovejoy. Well, I like that. And I suppose you think because you're My Lady Maypole you've bought the earth. Well, you haven't, see ? Because I've bought this bit.

Lady Maydew. Not altogether.

Mrs. Lovejoy. I've got the documents if you want to see them.

Lady Maydew. You will remember that the price of this cottage was five hundred pounds. You paid four hundred pounds. A hundred pounds is still owing.

Mrs. Lovejoy. To be paid in one month, all sealed and settled according to law.

Lady Maydew. Precisely. The cottage is yours when you pay.

Mrs. Lovejoy. I suppose you think we can't. Well, we can. You'll be sorry to hear we're doing very well.

Lady Maydew. I think we know how to deal with people like you in this district. You come here from the slums of the town, and you put up vile notices and commercialise the village, and you attract hordes of vulgar, ill-mannered people to trespass on my estate. Well, I think we can put a stop to that.

MRS. LOVEJOY. Oh, you can, can you?

LADY MAYDEW. I shall teach you a lesson you won't forget. You may be interested to hear that Wishton Hill, and the woods, and all the footpaths have been closed this morning by my orders. My keepers will deal severely with trespassers.

MRS. LOVEJOY (*deliberately*). I think you'd better take yourself out of here. You're defacing the beauty of my kitchen.

LOVEJOY. Now, ma, be quiet.

MRS. LOVEJOY. I won't be quiet. What does she mean coming in here talking like that?

LADY MAYDEW. All right, my good woman . . .

MRS. LOVEJOY. Good woman yourself!

LADY MAYDEW. That's quite enough.

MRS. LOVEJOY. Yes, it is. Quite enough. You'd better go now. You've outstayed your welcome.

(LADY MAYDEW *moves indignantly towards the door.*)

Oh, there's a lot more I can say to you if you want to hear it. Coming here dressed up like the Queen of the May, and casting aspersions on my notice . . .

(LADY MAYDEW *goes.*)

Good day to you!

(*She calls after* LADY MAYDEW.)

Good riddance to bad rubbish!

LOVEJOY. Now, ma, you shouldn't have said that.

MRS. LOVEJOY. I've not had much help from you, have I?

BETTY. Mother, is it true about the hundred pounds?

MRS. LOVEJOY. Yes. I had to keep some in hand for capital expenses.

LOVEJOY. You mean we've got a mortgage?

MRS. LOVEJOY. Call it that if you like. We'll soon pay it off out of profits.

LOVEJOY. I don't like it. Mortgages is bad. Pay as you go's my motto.

BETTY. But did you hear what she said about closing the woods? It can't be true.

JOE. We're sunk if she does that.

BETTY. People won't stop here at all. They'll go on to Winnerton.

MRS. LOVEJOY. She daren't do it. There's a public right of way. Has been for years.

Lovejoy. I don't like it. Getting mixed up with that sort of people. They can do a lot of harm.

Mrs. Lovejoy. Oo! I nearly lost my temper with her. Come on, now. It won't do no good talking about it. We'll have the people here before we know where we are. Father, go and get three pounds of butter from Mrs. Brownlow. The money's on the table. And don't stand gossiping with that woman. Joe, all those tables has got to be set up in the garden. (*To* Lovejoy.) Go on with you! Three pounds of butter. Can you keep it in your head or shall I write it down? And if you're not back in two minutes you'll hear about it.

Lovejoy (*memorising*). Three pounds of butter. You know, we ought to keep a cow.

(*He goes out.*)

Joe (*following him*). What for? You can't get butter from a cow.

(Mrs. Lovejoy *looks at a jam-pot.*)

Mrs. Lovejoy. Here, who's been at my jam?

(Joe *turns, looking sheepish, wiping his mouth.*)

Have *you*?

Joe. There was a fly in it, ma, so I took it out.

Mrs. Lovejoy. Fly? There's half a pot gone. Get out before I leather you!

(Joe *goes quickly.*)

Eating up my profits like that.

Betty. Do you think Lady Maydew really will close her estate?

Mrs. Lovejoy. The old—witch.

Betty. But it's very serious for us, if she does.

Mrs. Lovejoy. It's going to take more than her to beat me.

(Betty *starts arranging flowers in vases.*)

Betty. We can't fail now. We'd never be able to face up in the town again. And what'll become of us if things go wrong?

Mrs. Lovejoy. Things aren't going to go wrong. I know that. My birthday horoscope in the *News Herald* said " This will be a lucky year for you, with occasional annoyance, but in the end your dreams will come true." Here it is.

(*She shows* Betty *a newspaper cutting.*)

Betty (*reading*). " With occasional annoyance."

Mrs. Lovejoy. That means your father. We'll be all right.

(*There is a knock at the door. A bespectacled and adenoidal* GIRL *enters.*)

Well, and what do you want?

GIRL. If you please I'm the groceries.

MRS. LOVEJOY. Oh, are you? Well, where are they?

GIRL. Are you Mrs. Lovejoy?

MRS. LOVEJOY. I am.

GIRL. Well, my father says he's sorry but he hasn't got none of the things you ordered.

BETTY. What? No sugar and no tea?

GIRL. No, he's very sorry.

MRS. LOVEJOY. But he calls himself a grocer. And what about all the other things? I saw them in the shop.

GIRL. He's very sorry but he can't oblige.

BETTY. Why not?

GIRL. He says he's very sorry . . .

MRS. LOVEJOY. He'll be sorry before I've done with him.

BETTY. Doesn't he trust us? Tell him we'll pay at the door.

GIRL. It's not that. He says he's very sorry, though.

BETTY. Well, what is it?

GIRL. I don't know. I'm sorry, too. Good morning.

(*She goes.*)

MRS. LOVEJOY. Ah, the girl's daft. I'll have to go down and see for myself. Must be some misunderstanding.

BETTY. But he can't be out of stock of everything.

(MRS. LOVEJOY *puts on her hat.*)

MRS. LOVEJOY. It's these country-folk. Too much inter-marriaging in the country, that's what it is.

(*As she goes to the door* JOE *comes running in, pleased and excited.*)

JOE. I say, what do you think?

MRS. LOVEJOY. What?

JOE. Good news!

(*He rubs his hands.*)

BETTY. What is it?

JOE. There's been an accident!

MRS. LOVEJOY. Accident!

JOE. Young fellow turned his car over at the end of the road. I've got the job of putting it right. Two bent wings and a leaky radiator.

BETTY. Is he badly hurt?

JOE. No. Landed on his head, but he's all right. I asked

him if I could do the job just as he was coming round and he said " Yes."

Mrs. Lovejoy. Where is he ?

Joe. He's out there. (*He points to the garden.*) I let him sit down in the garden.

Mrs. Lovejoy. Well, bring him inside.

Joe. Shall I ?

Betty (*going to door*). Of course.

Joe (*calling*). Hey ! Come inside.

(Betty *goes out.* Joe *speaks to his mother.*)

Worth about a quid, this job, if it's worth a penny.

Mrs. Lovejoy (*at the window*). Oh, the poor lad ! You ought to have brought him in right away.

(Betty *appears supporting a young man. He is tall and good-looking He wears flannel trousers and a sports coat. He reels a bit and passes his hand over his head.* Mrs. Lovejoy *gets a chair.*)

T-t-t-t ! What a shame ! Here, sit down.

The Man. All right, thanks. Just got a bump on the head and it's made me feel giddy. Thanks.

Mrs. Lovejoy. Look at that. Bump the size of a hen's egg. Where's that butter ? Have we any left ?

Betty. There it is.

(Mrs. Lovejoy *gets butter and applies it to the back of his head.* Betty *examines his torn sleeve.*)

Just look at your sleeve. And look, your arm's all bleeding. Take your coat off.

(Betty *gets hot water and a bandage. He takes off his coat with the assistance of* Mrs. Lovejoy.)

Mrs. Lovejoy. It's my opinion you young fellows has no right to ride in cars at all. You ought to be in perambulators, some of you.

The Man. As a matter of fact it was your notice. I was so interested in it I took my eyes off the road and ran up the bank.

Joe. Ah ! That shows what a good notice it is.

Mrs. Lovejoy. Seems to be causing a lot of trouble this morning. I wish that Lady Maydew had fallen on her head when she saw the notice.

The Man. Lady Maydew ? Has she been here ?

Mrs. Lovejoy. She has that. But she won't come again in a hurry. I told her where she got off. She isn't a friend of yours, is she ?

THE MAN. Well, I have met her. (*He smiles.*) Did she object to the notice ?

BETTY (*applying the bandage*). Keep still, please.

MRS. LOVEJOY. Yes, she did. But that notice stays where it is, and I wouldn't take it down not for the King of China himself.

THE MAN. There aren't many people who stand up to Lady Maydew and live to tell the tale.

MRS. LOVEJOY. No, she's never met *me* before.

BETTY. You'll have to sit still if you want me to do this properly.

THE MAN. I'm sorry. It's very good of you to take all this trouble. I'm quite all right now, really I am.

MRS. LOVEJOY (*with a cup of tea*). If that woman or any of her kind come here again I won't be answerable for what happens to them. Have a cup of tea.

THE MAN. Thanks.

JOE. I'm going to start on that job.

THE MAN. That's right. When will it be ready ?

JOE. To-night. About eight.

THE MAN. That's splendid.

(JOE *goes out.* THE MAN *looks at his bandage.*)

I say, you've done that terribly well. Thanks very much.

BETTY. Drink your tea and you'll feel better. Put your jacket on first.

(*She helps him.*)

THE MAN. I think you'd make rather a good nurse. You've got the habit of ordering people about.

BETTY. Some people need ordering about.

THE MAN. Meaning me, I suppose ?

BETTY. Yes, I was thinking of you. You want to look where you're going when you drive a car. Men like you are worse than babies.

(THE MAN *laughs.*)

MRS. LOVEJOY. Don't be rude to the gentleman, Betty. He's probably not used to it.

THE MAN. Oh, I rather like it. (*To* BETTY.) So your name's Betty, is it ?

BETTY. Yes, why ?

THE MAN. Oh . . . it's rather a nice name, isn't it ?

BETTY. Do you think so ?

THE MAN. Yes.

(*They look at each other. He is smiling, she is puzzled.*)

Mrs. Lovejoy. Here, young man, if you've nothing better to do than bandy words with my daughter, and you're feeling all right, you'd better go.

The Man. I say, there seems to be a lot of plain speaking in this house. But I'm very grateful to you. (*He rises.*) Sorry to have been a nuisance. And, look here, I'll be back for the car about eight. (*To* Betty.) Is that all right?

Betty. As far as I know it is. Joe looks after the garage.

The Man. I see. Well, perhaps I'll see you when I call. (*He holds his arm.*) This may have taken a turn for the worse.

Betty. I should see a doctor if it does.

The Man (*snubbed*). Oh? Well, good morning—and thanks very much.

(*He goes.*)

Mrs. Lovejoy. Hum! Seems a cheeky young fellow.

Betty. I don't know. I think he's rather nice.

Mrs. Lovejoy. Oh, do you? So that's what brought the red in your cheeks, is it?

Betty. Mother, don't!

Mrs. Lovejoy. You be careful if he calls again. I don't trust fellows who talk all nice and B.B.C. first time they meet a young woman.

(Mrs. Lovejoy *is laying the table for the mid-day meal.*)

Pass me those plates. I'll have to see the grocer after dinner.

Betty. He must live round here, if he's leaving his car and coming back for it.

(Lovejoy *appears. He is worried and breathless.* Joe *follows.*)

Lovejoy. I say, ma.

Mrs. Lovejoy. What's wrong now? Where's the butter?

Lovejoy. I haven't got any.

Mrs. Lovejoy. Not got any?

Lovejoy. Listen a minute. They're putting up fences all over the place, and notices with " Trespassers will be Prosecuted " on them.

Betty. Have they closed Wishton Hill?

Lovejoy. Aye, they have that.

Joe. They've got keepers all over the place.

Mrs. Lovejoy. That's bad.

Lovejoy. And that's not all. Mrs. Brownlow wouldn't serve me with butter.

Betty. Why not?

Lovejoy. Orders from Lady Maydew that nobody in the

village is to serve us with anything. They'll be turned out if they do.

MRS. LOVEJOY (*dumbfounded*). Well . . .

BETTY. That's why the groceries didn't come. She's been at them too.

LOVEJOY. I reckon it's about finished us and our little plans.

MRS. LOVEJOY. It hasn't. Don't you go talking like that.

BETTY. What can we do ?

MRS. LOVEJOY. Do ? We can fight !

LOVEJOY. How are you going to fight, ma ?

MRS. LOVEJOY. I don't know yet. But I do know this. (*She flourishes a knife.*) From now on it's War—War to the death on Lady Maydew and all her kind ! Come on—sit down and get your dinners.

CURTAIN.

SCENE 2. *The same. Evening of the same Saturday. The food and crockery at the back remains untouched.* LOVEJOY, *in his shirt-sleeves, wearing a bowler hat and a white apron, sits smoking and reading the paper. He turns to look anxiously through the window, and then resumes his reading.* MRS. LOVEJOY *darns socks by the fireplace.*

LOVEJOY. Betty still out yonder ?

MRS. LOVEJOY. Yes.

(*He reads again.*)

LOVEJOY. She might as well come in now. Nearly eight o'clock, ma. Nobody'll want tea at this time of night.

(*There is a silence.*)

It's been a bad day for us.

(MRS. LOVEJOY *darns furiously.*)

Would you like to go for a bit of a walk ?

MRS. LOVEJOY. Oh, hush with you ! I feel that mad I daren't trust myself to speak.

LOVEJOY. But you aren't mad at me, ma ?

MRS. LOVEJOY. No, but *you'll* get it.

(LOVEJOY *rises and scratches his head.*)

LOVEJOY (*indicating his apron*). I suppose I can take this off now.

Mrs. Lovejoy. Yes. And I don't see why you want to go wearing your hat in the house.

Lovejoy. I've always worn a hat when I've been working, ma, and I can't think proper without it.

Mrs. Lovejoy. I never thought you up to much with it on.

Lovejoy. Now, ma, come on, let's go for a walk. It won't do you no good sitting brooding over it all. Try and forget that Lady Maydew and all her " Trespassers will be Prosecuted."

Mrs. Lovejoy. Aye, but I can't forget all that food we've brought in. It's going to be a dead loss to us. Nobody'll ever stop here now the woods is closed. What have we had to-day? A Boy Scout asking for hot water, and two cyclists who wanted tea and brought their own sandwiches.

Lovejoy. Come on, now. Put your hat on. We'll take a walk.

Mrs. Lovejoy (*rising*). Oh, all right. Though if we do meet that Lady Maydew I won't be responsible for anything that might happen.

(Betty *enters. She wears a smart coloured apron for her duties in the tea-garden. She carries a pile of tablecloths.* Mrs. Lovejoy *puts on her hat and coat.* Lovejoy *puts on his jacket.*)

Betty. I brought these in. There's a heavy dew rising.

Lovejoy. Now, lass, buck up! Don't look so downhearted. What was it you said to me that night as mother bought the cottage? " Striking out into the west like settlers in covered wagons . . ." That's what you said. Well, settlers had a deal more than this to put up with.

Mrs. Lovejoy. They didn't have notices up with " Trespassers will be Prosecuted." We're going out for a stroll, Betty. Is Joe still working?

Betty. Yes. He's nearly finished. Just a minute, dad.

(*She adjusts his hat a bit over one eye.*)

That's better.

Lovejoy. Here, what's that for?

Betty. That's how I like it.

(Mrs. Lovejoy *goes out.*)

Mrs. Lovejoy. Come on, father.

Lovejoy (*glancing in a mirror*). Aach! You're always messing me about.

Betty. Go on, you look a regular swell.

Lovejoy. Do I, Betty?

(*He chuckles and follows* Mrs. Lovejoy.)

Coming, ma, coming!

(BETTY *brings a lighted oil lamp from a side table to the* c. *table. Then she gets out her cash-book and pen and ink. She counts out a small quantity of loose change and sighs. Then she sits and writes.* THE MAN *looks in at the window and knocks at the door. It is growing dark outside.*)

BETTY. Who's there?
THE MAN. May I come in?

(*He enters.*)

BETTY. Oh, it's you. Your car's at the garage. Not in here.
THE MAN. Yes, it's not quite ready. I thought I'd just come in and say " how d'you do?"
BETTY. I'm very busy.
THE MAN (*crestfallen*). I see. I'm sorry. Er, good night.

(*He goes. She calls.*)

BETTY. I say . . . I don't mind you sitting down if you'll keep quiet.

(*He returns.*)

THE MAN. Sure it's all right?
BETTY (*pointing to a chair*). Sit there.
THE MAN. Oh, thanks.

(*He sits and puts his cap on the table.* BETTY *writes. She speaks without looking up.*)

BETTY. How's your arm?
THE MAN. Fine, thanks. I did wonder if perhaps it ought to be dressed.
BETTY. Did you? Haven't you anybody at home? Your wife?
THE MAN. I'm not married.
BETTY (*looking uninterested*). Aren't you really? Your mother, then?
THE MAN (*smiling*). No . . . I don't think she'd bother about a scratch like that.
BETTY. Then you can't expect me to bother, can you?
THE MAN. Well, no. (*A pause.*) Homework?

(*He indicates her account book.*)

BETTY (*tossing her head*). Don't be silly. These are accounts.
THE MAN. Do you run this business?
BETTY. I look after the financial side. You have to be business-like—even about a tea-garden.
THE MAN. And how is business?

BETTY. Bad.

THE MAN. I'm sorry. How's that?

BETTY. Oh, it's that Lady Whats-her-name.

THE MAN. Maydew?

BETTY. That's it. Do you know her?

THE MAN (*with a smile*). I've—met her. What's *she* done?

BETTY. Oo, I'd like to . . . But perhaps she's a friend of yours?

THE MAN. Come on, tell me what she's done, and what you'd like to do to her?

BETTY. First of all she objected to our notice. Then she's given instructions that nobody must serve us with any goods. And worst of all she's closed all the paths and the woods and put up notices all over the place. Nobody'll come here any more.

THE MAN. That's why she's done it, is it?

BETTY. You've seen them?

THE MAN. Yes. But I didn't know it was for your benefit.

BETTY. She said this morning she'd teach us a lesson. I suppose she has done.

THE MAN (*rising and walking angrily about*). Gosh! It's positively mediæval. She'd no right to do a thing like that.

BETTY. Do you live round here?

THE MAN. Not far away.

BETTY. Where?

THE MAN. Just over the hill. Look here, I feel very deeply about this business. I wish I could explain—but I don't quite know what to do. You see, these old families hold the land. Antiquated property laws, and all that sort of thing. But they really hold it in trust, for the people. It's the people's land—that's what's we've got to realise. And we've got to keep up with the times. Nowadays the people live in towns, and have bicycles and motor cars, and we've no right to stop them using their own countryside.

BETTY. What can we do?

THE MAN. If I was one of the people from the town I'd smash down the fences and pull up the notices and I'd raise hell if anybody tried to keep me off the land—off " England's green and pleasant land."

BETTY. You're a bit of a red, aren't you?

THE MAN. Ah, it makes me boil! Something's got to be done.

BETTY. Anyway, it mayn't be all her fault. They say in the village it's young Sir Gerald.

THE MAN. Oh? What do they say about him?

BETTY. Is he a friend of yours?

THE MAN (*fiercely*). Never mind. Tell me what they say?

BETTY. Don't shout, please.

THE MAN. I'm sorry. I want to know what they say about —about Sir Gerald Maydew.

BETTY. They say he's weak, and let's his mother have all her own way with tenants. He's over twenty-one and he won't take any interest in his estate. And they say he's a lazy good-for-nothing, and not fit to be a country squire at all. I'd like to meet him.

THE MAN. Would you ? Why ?

BETTY. I'd tell him a thing or two.

THE MAN. Such as ?

BETTY. I'd ask him why he puts up barbed wire and notices on land that's been open to the public for generations. I'd ask him why he lets people like us be victimised by her blessed ladyship—stopping the tenants supplying us—doing her best to hound us out of the village.

THE MAN. Go on.

BETTY. I'd ask him why he doesn't *do* something instead of idling round like people say. He could sell half his land and turn his house into a hotel. It's near the main road.

THE MAN (*with a smile*). I don't think anybody's ever spoken to him like that before. Perhaps you ought to tell him a thing or two. A hotel's not a bad idea.

BETTY. And if ever you meet him, you can tell him what I say.

(*She goes up to the window.*)

THE MAN. I certainly will.

BETTY. Look—the moon's rising.

(*He follows her.*)

THE MAN. " The deep of night has crept upon our talk."

BETTY. That's rather nice. " The deep of night has crept upon our talk." Particularly as I had no intention of talking to you at all.

THE MAN. Are you glad you came to the country ?

BETTY. Glad ! It's wonderful ! You've never lived in a town, have you ?

THE MAN. Not long. I was at Oxford three years.

BETTY. Were you really ? Still, I don't think Oxford's like the town I come from—all streets and mills and chimneys. That's why the country feels so grand, with the smell of hay and the flowers. I've never seen such flowers. No wonder the country folk want to keep it all to themselves.

THE MAN. The country belongs to those who love it.

BETTY. Do *you* ?

The Man (*quietly*). Never so deeply as I do at this moment. I feel that I love it so much that if I were from the town, and they tried to keep me out of those woods up there, with the moon rising over them—I'd pull down their fences for them. And if I went to prison for it, I'd be glad because I'd done it for freedom.

Betty. Is that what you learned at Oxford?

The Man (*laughing*). Perhaps I learned it from you. I've never felt like this before.

Betty. Well, this sort of thing won't do. Standing talking to customers in the moonlight. I'd better light the lamp.

(*She takes some matches and stands on a chair to light the lamp hanging over the table. He helps her.*)

The Man. Here, let me do that.

Betty. I can manage, thanks.

(*He stands on another chair.*)

The Man. Here you are. Here's a match.

(*They are lighting the lamp, when* Joe *comes in.* The Man *seems to be unnecessarily close to* Betty.)

Joe. Hello? What's up? (*To* The Man.) Your car's ready.

The Man. Oh, is it? Thank you. I'll come now.

(*They still stand on chairs.*)

Well, good night. Perhaps I'll see you again.

Betty. Perhaps you will. Good night.

(*They shake hands.* The Man *gets down and goes with* Joe.)

Joe. You'd better have a look at the front wheels. I think they're out of alignment.

The Man. Right, we'll take her for a run.

(*They go.* Betty *gets down from her chair and looks out of the window as she draws the curtains. Then she comes back to her writing at the table. She bites her pen.* Mrs. Lovejoy *returns from her walk.*)

Mrs. Lovejoy. Oh? So he came again, did he?

Betty. Yes.

(Mrs. Lovejoy *hangs up her hat and coat.*)

Mrs. Lovejoy. Did *you* ask him in?

Betty. He just came in for a talk.

Mrs. Lovejoy. And what did you talk about?

BETTY.   Lots of things.

(*She smiles.*)

MRS. LOVEJOY.   So that's why you're looking so cheerful. Come on, lass, tell me all about him.

BETTY.   I don't know very much. He's been to Oxford.

MRS. LOVEJOY.   Oxford ? That's a good school, isn't it ?

BETTY.   It's a university.

MRS. LOVEJOY.   That explains his queer way of talking. Poor lad !

BETTY.   He seems to know the people at the Hall. But he's on our side about the fences. Wanted to smash them down.

MRS. LOVEJOY.   Did he ?

(LOVEJOY *enters and stands listening.*)

Sounds the right sort to me. What's his name ?

BETTY.   I don't know. He didn't tell me.

LOVEJOY (*coming forward*).   Oh, didn't he ?

BETTY.   I never asked him.

LOVEJOY.   More fool you. You watch your step, my lass. I know that sort of toffy chap, here to-day and gone to-morrow, and buzzing round a pretty face like a bee round an 'oney-pot.

MRS. LOVEJOY.   Oh, go on, George. Betty can look after herself. He came for his car.

LOVEJOY.   Aye, but I saw him coming out of here. And whose cap's that on the table ?

BETTY.   He must have left it.

LOVEJOY.   Aye, they always do. He wants to come again. He's not your class, and no good ever came of climbing social barriers. I expect he tried to kiss you.

BETTY.   He did nothing of the sort !

LOVEJOY.   Well, he will next time. But he won't tell you his name—not him. Then one of these days you'll be wanting his name *and* his address.

MRS. LOVEJOY.   Father ! How could you ?

LOVEJOY.   I know.

(*There is a knock on the door.*)

MRS. LOVEJOY.   See who that is, Betty.

(BETTY *goes to the door. A man's voice asks for* MRS. LOVEJOY.)

BETTY.   Yes, she's in. Do you want to speak to her. (*She turns to her mother.*) A Mr. Robinson. He says he's from the Hall.

MRS. LOVEJOY.   Mr. Robinson ? Oh, yes, that's him that I bought the cottage from. Tell him to come in.

BETTY. Come in, please, Mr. Robinson.

(ROBINSON, *a private estate agent, enters. He is dressed in riding-
breeches.*)

ROBINSON. Good evening, Mrs. Lovejoy. You remember me
—agent for the Maydew Hall estate.

MRS. LOVEJOY. Yes, I won't forget you in a hurry, you old
Shylock. You drove a hard bargain with me over this cottage,
didn't you ?

ROBINSON. Well, no, Mrs. Lovejoy, I think you got very
favourable terms. Specially when you consider I nearly lost my
job for selling it at all.

MRS. LOVEJOY. You never told me about Lady Maydew.

ROBINSON. No, she was away at the time. Unfortunately I
acted on young Sir Gerald's instructions when I sold the cottage.
You see, it's this way. He and his mother don't see eye to eye
about the estate. She's old-fashioned and wants to keep it like
it's always been, which is very difficult when the estate's near
bankrupt. Now young Sir Gerald's different—he's got queer
ideas—he's by way of being a socialist, and I think he'd get rid
of the whole estate if he could.

LOVEJOY. Aye, but what's all this got to do with us ?

ROBINSON. I'm coming to that. I'm afraid I've got bad news
for you, Mrs. Lovejoy. Her ladyship sent for me to-night, and
she says if the money that's owing on this cottage isn't paid by
next Thursday, which was the day arranged, you'll get notice
to quit.

MRS. LOVEJOY. Well, we won't go.

ROBINSON. I'll lose my job if you don't. And if you force me
to it I'll have to turn you out.

LOVEJOY. You see, ma, I told you it was doing no good talking
like you did to her. You should have kept a civil tongue in your
head.

BETTY. Why does Sir Gerald let her behave like this to us ?
Can't he do anything ?

ROBINSON. Well, between you and me, he's never had a
chance. She's kept a tight hand on everything, and he's never
had a say in managing the estate. She won't let him.

BETTY. I'd kick him round. Why doesn't he stand up to
her ?

ROBINSON. Maybe he will one of these days. But she *is* his
mother, you know. Well, Mrs. Lovejoy, that's what I came to
tell you. I've had my instructions and I'm very sorry about it.
I'll say good night.

MRS. LOVEJOY. Good night. And if you meet young baronet
tell him from me I don't wonder he's a socialist, living with Lady

Maydew. I only had five minutes of her and I'm a ruddy Bolshevik.

Lovejoy. Steady on, ma. You mustn't say things like that.

Robinson. Well, that's how it is. Good night.

(*He goes.* Mrs. Lovejoy *sits down grimly by the table, drumming with her hand on it.*)

Betty (*to her mother*). I've a good mind to go to the Hall and talk to them myself.

Lovejoy. Now then, Betty, leave your mother alone when she's like that.

Betty. Something's got to be done.

Lovejoy. We can't do anything by talking wild. Property laws have got to be respected. I'm a constitutionalist whatever happens.

Mrs. Lovejoy. Of course I suppose you're all blaming me now for bringing you into the country.

Lovejoy. Nay, I reckon it were my idea as much as anyone else's.

Betty. We aren't blaming you at all, mother. But we must do something.

Mrs. Lovejoy. Joe's garage cost a deal more than I expected.

Lovejoy. If the worst happens I can always go back to the town.

Betty. So can I. My job's still open.

Mrs. Lovejoy. We can't go back now. It's the disgrace.

Lovejoy. Seems to me we're in disgrace wherever we are.

Betty. We *can* get a bit of our own back.

Lovejoy. How?

(*She looks through the window.*)

Betty. Is that young fellow still there?

Lovejoy. He's down in the garage with Joe.

(Betty *picks up his cap and goes.*)

Here, where you going?

Betty. I'll be back soon.

(*She goes out.*)

Lovejoy. What's our Betty up to?

Mrs. Lovejoy. Don't ask me.

Lovejoy. I hope she's not taken on with that young fellow.

Mrs. Lovejoy. I don't know. She might do worse.

Lovejoy. You want to be careful of these country folk. They see too much of farmyards to have any proper morals.

Mrs. Lovejoy. I don't make much of 'em. Not that any of them'll speak to us. They've all been warned off.

Lovejoy. They're all frightened, that's what they are. When I went into Rose and Crown last night I might have had typhoid fever the way they cold-shouldered me.

(*He has put his tool-bag on the table, and he is rubbing a saw with an oily rag.*)

Mrs. Lovejoy. What you doing with them things on the table ?

Lovejoy. Them things ! The way things are going, missus, I'll be needing them afore long. I'll have to get a job.

(BETTY *returns, followed by the young man and* JOE.)

What's to do now ?

Betty (*to* THE MAN). Come right inside.

The Man (*nodding to* MR. *and* MRS. LOVEJOY). Good evening.

Lovejoy. What have you brought that in for ?

Mrs. Lovejoy. What's up, lass ?

Betty. I've got a plan.

Lovejoy. Huh ! We've had enough plans in this family.

Betty. Listen, all of you. I know that what I'm going to suggest is against the law, but if we just sit down under something that isn't just we're doing wrong. Well, I'm not going to sit down.

Mrs. Lovejoy. I don't know what you're talking about.

Lovejoy. Betty, you're excited.

Betty. Yes, I am. (*To* THE MAN.) Didn't you tell me just now about antiquated property laws ?

The Man (*smiling*). I believe I did.

Betty. Didn't you say that if anybody tried to keep you off the land you'd pull down their notice-boards and smash up their fences ?

The Man. Yes. I said something like that.

Betty. Well, we've been kept off the land round here. I say it's unjust, and I'm going out now to smash up Lady Maydew's fences. Will you help me ?

Mrs. Lovejoy }
Lovejoy   } (*together*).   Nay, lass . . .
                                 Don't talk rubbish !

The Man. You don't mean that.

Betty. Yes I do.

Joe (*eagerly*). Right ! I'll come with you.

Lovejoy. Here, steady on, Joe.

The Man. You're not serious ?

Betty. Of course I'm serious. The land's been closed. They're trying to ruin us, and now they're going to turn us out.

THE MAN. I don't think we can do much good.

BETTY. So you didn't mean what you said?

THE MAN. I was speaking in a general way. I meant a concerted movement on the part of the community as a whole.

BETTY. This is a concerted movement—you and me and Joe.

LOVEJOY. Here, Betty, steady on, steady on.

BETTY (to THE MAN). Didn't you say you'd go to prison and be glad because you'd struck a blow for freedom?

THE MAN. I said something of the sort.

BETTY. Didn't you mean it?

THE MAN. I—well . . . I was perhaps suggesting an ideological rather than a practical course of action under the circumstances.

BETTY. Oh, you lovely talker! Don't they teach you nice words at Oxford? Well, you're going to *do* something for a change, young man.

THE MAN. Here, you're not seriously . . .

BETTY. Yes, I am, and you're coming too.

THE MAN. But . . .

MRS. LOVEJOY. Now, Betty, you're getting a bit above yourself.

BETTY. Don't you see, mother, we've got to do something to hit back. We'll show Lady Maydew what we think of her.

(JOE *has produced a large axe.*)

JOE. Will this do?

BETTY. That's splendid!

LOVEJOY. The girl's taken leave of her senses.

BETTY. You can come too, father.

LOVEJOY. Me come! Well, I'm not going. And neither are you.

BETTY. Oh, yes we are. Come on, Joe. I want a big pair of pliers.

(*She looks at* THE MAN.)

Of course, if you're afraid . . .

THE MAN. I think your father's right.

BETTY. You're not a coward, are you?

THE MAN. Certainly not.

BETTY. Then come on.

(JOE *leads the way.* BETTY *pushes* THE MAN *out and follows.*)

LOVEJOY. Here, come back! Come back! You can't do things like that. Mother, why don't you tell that lass to come back?

MRS. LOVEJOY. She didn't take much notice of *you*, did she?

LOVEJOY. You're not letting her go ?

MRS. LOVEJOY (*smiling—she still sits beside the table*). I'm glad to see the lass has got a bit of me in her. Happen I ought to have gone too.

LOVEJOY. Do you think there's any good ever came of pulling down private property? It won't do none of us any good. Here, I'm going to fetch her back.

(*He puts on his hat and makes for the door.* MRS. LOVEJOY *picks up his saw from the table.*)

MRS. LOVEJOY. George?

LOVEJOY. What is it?

MRS. LOVEJOY. I've got a little plan. If I was cutting through a post I'd hold it like that, wouldn't I?

LOVEJOY. Now what you going to do? You and your little plans !

MRS. LOVEJOY (*picking up another saw*). Or would I use this one?

LOVEJOY. You'd want a cross-cut for going across the grain. This one. Here, what's the idea?

MRS. LOVEJOY. If you was to go quietly up to a notice-board and saw—like that—right through the post. You'd be good at it, George, you being a skilled carpenter.

LOVEJOY. Well, I'll be damned !

MRS. LOVEJOY. And there, see—a pair of wire-cutters. Just what we want.

LOVEJOY. What for? You can't expect me to go behaving unlawful. There's no sense in it.

MRS. LOVEJOY (*putting away the tools*). No, there isn't really, is there, George? You always were a sensible one. Well, happen you'd best go out and stop Betty doing anything unlawful.

LOVEJOY. Right, I will. (*He turns.*) And think on, now, ma. No nonsense.

MRS. LOVEJOY. No, George.

(*He goes. Then she watches him through the curtain. She puts on her hat, picks up the saw and wire-cutters and goes out after him.*)

CURTAIN.

SCENE 3. *The same—two hours later. The lamp still burns and the* LOVEJOYS *have not yet returned. The door is slightly ajar, and an owl is heard hooting outside. Then a police whistle blows. Voices are heard, and there is a loud knocking on the door.*)

ROBINSON'S VOICE. Is there anybody in?

LADY MAYDEW's VOICE. Don't be a fool, Robinson ! Of course there's nobody in.

(LADY MAYDEW *enters, followed by* ROBINSON.)

Hello ?

(*She calls upstairs.*)

Is there anybody here ? There you are. That proves it. These people have done all the mischief.

(*The Police whistle blows again.*)

ROBINSON. There it is again, my lady.
LADY MAYDEW. There's what again ?
ROBINSON. It sounded like a police whistle.
LADY MAYDEW. It probably was a police whistle, Robinson. Where are your men ?
ROBINSON. Kirby and Waters are on the north side of the woods. Jordan and the gardeners are watching this side. I left Sergeant Bennett on the south side.

(*The whistle again, very close.*)

LADY MAYDEW. You're sure they're in the wood ?
ROBINSON. Sure of it, my lady.
LADY MAYDEW. Well, this proves what I said. The house is empty. They're responsible for the damage.

(*A* POLICE SERGEANT *appears at the door.*)

SERGEANT. Did you see him ?
LADY MAYDEW. See who ?
SERGEANT. Young fellow, your ladyship. And I think there was a young woman with him. I chased him from the woods but he gave me the slip.
LADY MAYDEW. They're certainly not in here. Go along, man, find them. And stop blowing that whistle.
SERGEANT. All the notice-boards have been sawn down, Mr. Robinson.
ROBINSON. Sawn down ?
LADY MAYDEW. Precisely. This man is a carpenter. See there's his tool-bag. Please hurry—I want to catch them red-handed. Sergeant, you go back to the woods. Robinson, you watch the road.
ROBINSON. Yes, my lady.

(*They go out. There is silence for a time and then the window on the* R. *is pushed open and* THE MAN *climbs through. He turns and helps* BETTY *through the window.*)

THE MAN. Are you all right?

BETTY. Yes, I'm all right. I wonder where Joe is?

THE MAN. He was in the wood—but he ran the other way.

BETTY. Keep away from the window. They may be watching. I say—we haven't half done it, have we?

THE MAN. We made a good job of the wire, anyway. (*He laughs.*) I say, you don't know how funny this is!

BETTY. You can laugh now, but you were scared enough when you saw the keepers. Turn round.

(*She inspects him from behind.*)

I thought so.

(*She gets her workbasket.*)

THE MAN. Please don't bother. Look here, your people won't like me coming in at this time.

BETTY. Don't worry about them. They've gone to bed. They'll be sleeping peacefully.

THE MAN. You know, you don't know what you've done for me.

BETTY. For you?

THE MAN (*he laughs*). Making *me* cut that wire. I feel a lot better for it. I've cut through something else as well.

BETTY (*threading a needle*). I don't know quite what you mean. Is this more ideology—or whatever you call it?

THE MAN. Look here, I do admire you. I admire your courage. And well, I admire quite a lot of things about you . . . Betty . . .

BETTY. Do you really? You've been very helpful. Bend over.

THE MAN. I wanted to say . . .

BETTY. This way, please.

(*He bends over and she sews his trousers.*)

I'm really very grateful to you. I admire you, too.

THE MAN. Do you?

(*He jumps as the needle pricks him.*)

BETTY. I shall hurt you if you jump.

THE MAN (*bending again*). Sorry.

(*She sews.*)

What I really want to say is this. If you found out anything about me that made me seem to be different from what you think I am—you'd still think the same about me—I mean, we'd still get on together, wouldn't we? '

BETTY. Say that again.

THE MAN. It's rather difficult. I mean, supposing I wasn't what you think I am. . . .

BETTY. You haven't done a murder, have you?

THE MAN. No, nothing like that. I haven't been quite straight with you, that's all.

BETTY. You're not married?

THE MAN. Good lord, no.

BETTY. Please tell me.

THE MAN. There's something I want to say. But I can't say it like this.

BETTY. There you are. It's finished.

THE MAN. Thanks very much.

(*He stands upright.*)

BETTY. Now, what do you want to tell me?

THE MAN. I . . . Oh, well, it doesn't matter.

BETTY. I wonder why Joe doesn't come. I'm worried.

THE MAN. He'll be all right. Look here—this has been a wonderful night. And I've got a feeling it's all coming to an end. You aren't going to be so very pleased with me.

BETTY. Why not? I think you've been very brave, and helpful.

THE MAN. That's just it. I'm not brave. I'm just a fool.

BETTY. What is the matter?

THE MAN. Betty—I love you!

BETTY. Well, that's all right.

THE MAN. Is it?

BETTY. Yes.

THE MAN (*embracing her*). Darling!

BETTY. I suppose you know you haven't told me your name.

THE MAN. No, that's just it.

BETTY. You haven't forgotten it?

THE MAN. Promise me it won't make any difference.

BETTY. Why should it?

THE MAN. It happens to be Maydew.

BETTY. Maydew?

THE MAN. Yes. I'm Gerald Maydew. Those were my own fences I was cutting down to-night. So you see—I wasn't so brave as you thought I was. But I'm glad I did it all the same.

BETTY. You're Sir Gerald Maydew?

GERALD. Yes. I say, don't look at me like that.

BETTY. You're not having me on?

GERALD. Having you on? No, of course I'm not.

BETTY. Why didn't you tell me?

GERALD. Because it's not a thing that matters. I didn't think you were the sort of girl to be impressed.

BETTY. I'm not impressed.

GERALD. You certainly look it.

BETTY. No—I'm just sorry.

GERALD. Why sorry?

BETTY. I don't know. I rather liked you—and your funny way of talking. Well, it's all over now. You've had your little joke—I think you'd better go.

GERALD. But, damn it all, it isn't a joke! I'm perfectly serious. This is definitely a turning-point in my life. You remember what they said about me—weak and good-for-nothing —well, it's all true. Though it isn't going to be true any longer.

BETTY. Why?

GERALD. In future I'm going to manage my own estate.

BETTY. Funny way to start—cutting down your own fences.

GERALD. I know it's absurd, but cutting down that barbed wire to-night was symbolical. I've cut through my own barbed wire entanglements. You've done this for me.

BETTY. Me?

GERALD. Yes, you. You're the sort of girl who can make a chap do things—lift him out of the rut—and push him along. . . . Don't look at me like that—I'm trying to make love to you.

BETTY. You're not very good at it, *Sir Gerald*.

GERALD. Don't call me that. Look here, I do love you. Honestly. I know it's sudden—but it's pretty sure. . . .

BETTY. It seems to me you'll have to make up your mind which side of the fence you're really on. You can't have it both ways. Either you're one of us, or else you're Sir Gerald Maydew, and the owner of a big estate. I don't think my people would approve of you.

GERALD. Well, I should think I've been pretty democratic to-night.

(The police whistle blows distantly. MRS. LOVEJOY *runs in at the door, slams it and holds her weight against it. Someone hammers on the other side.)*

MRS. LOVEJOY. Here, Betty, quick! Give us a hand. Look, he's got his foot in.

BETTY. Mother!

MRS. LOVEJOY. It's the police!

(BETTY *looks through the window.)*

BETTY. No, it isn't. It's father!

(Mrs. Lovejoy *lets the door open and* Lovejoy *enters, closing the door behind him.*)

Mrs. Lovejoy. It's you, George . . .

Lovejoy. Of course it's me. (*He is breathless.*)

Mrs. Lovejoy. Was that you chased me down the lane ?

Lovejoy. Yes.

Mrs. Lovejoy. Why didn't you say so ?

Lovejoy. I hadn't any breath left. Ma, they're after us !

Mrs. Lovejoy. Well, we're safe enough now. (*To* Betty *and* Gerald.) We've sawn off all their signposts. All their " Trespassers will be Prosecuted." Not a blessed one left standing on the whole estate. Where's Joe.

Betty. We lost him.

Lovejoy. There you are, you see. Just like Joe if he goes and gets caught.

(*He puts his saw in the bag and puts it away.*)

It's the daftest business I were ever in. I think you all ought to be ashamed of yourselves.

Mrs. Lovejoy. Don't forget it was you did most of the sawing.

Lovejoy. Only because I couldn't bear to see the way you handled a saw. Might as well do the job proper even if it is against the law.

Mrs. Lovejoy. And what have you two been up to ?

Betty. He'd better explain.

Mrs. Lovejoy. Oh, there's summat to explain, is there ?

Lovejoy. Now what's wrong ?

Gerald. Well, there's nothing wrong. I think you've done terribly well, Mrs. Lovejoy, sawing down all those notice-boards. I congratulate you. We concentrated on the barbed wire. In fact I—(*he indicates his trousers*)—Betty's been sewing me up. That's why I'm here.

Betty. Isn't there something else ?

Gerald. Oh, yes, perhaps I ought to tell you. You may think it's rather queer, but this is my estate.

Lovejoy. What does he say ?

Betty. This is Lady Maydew's son, and the estate belongs to him.

Mrs. Lovejoy. You're Lady Maydew's son ?

Betty. He's Sir Gerald Maydew.

Mrs. Lovejoy. Why didn't he say so before ?

Lovejoy. You mean you've been cutting down fences on your own land ?

Gerald. Yes, sir, and I've thoroughly enjoyed it.

Lovejoy. You must be barmy !

(*A knock at the door.* Mrs. Lovejoy *opens it.*)

Mrs. Lovejoy. Oh, it's you. Come inside.

(Lady Maydew *enters.   She looks round and sees* Gerald.)

Lady Maydew. Gerald, what are you doing here ?
Gerald. Well, mother . . .
Lady Maydew. Do you know that a great deal of damage
has been done on the estate ? And by these people ?
Gerald. I think I can explain . . .
Lady Maydew. There is nothing to explain. (*She calls at the
door*). Robinson, bring him in.

(Robinson *and the* Sergeant *enter with* Joe *between them.*)

Well, here we are. Is this your son ?
Mrs. Lovejoy. He is.
Lady Maydew. I thought so. We caught him red-handed.
What was he doing, Robinson ?
Robinson (*holding up the axe*). We caught him in the act of
smashing up the newly-erected gate at the entrance to the woods
on the south side, my lady.
Lady Maydew. Quite so. And I don't think he's the only
one from this house who's been trespassing on the estate to-night.
Gerald. No, mother—I have.
Lady Maydew. What do you mean ?
Gerald. I mean I've been cutting down fences too.
Lady Maydew. Gerald, are you mad ?
Gerald. Robinson, let that boy go. Officer, I make no
charge against anybody. I'm sorry you've all been troubled.
Lady Maydew. What's the meaning of this ?
Gerald. I've decided to take no action in the matter.
Lady Maydew. Take no action ?
Mrs. Lovejoy. Do you mean we've cut down those notice-
boards for nothing ?
Lovejoy. Now then, ma, don't interfere.
Mrs. Lovejoy. But I'm going to interfere. This is a first-
class row and we haven't heard the end of it yet. Didn't she
try and turn me off her estate ? Didn't she try and ruin our
business and hound us out of the village ? This is going in the
papers. I've been in once and I'll go in again.
Lady Maydew. Do you propose to write to *The Times ?*
Mrs. Lovejoy. No, it's easier than that. (*She points to the*
Police Sergeant). Come here, you.
Sergeant (*coming forward*). What is it ?
Mrs. Lovejoy. Have you got a police station in the village ?
Sergeant. Of course we have.

MRS. LOVEJOY. Has it got a prison cell ?
SERGEANT. Yes, we've got a lock-up.
MRS. LOVEJOY. Right you are, then.

(*She knocks off the* SERGEANT'*s helmet.*)

SERGEANT. Here, steady on, steady on.
BETTY. Mother, don't do that !
LOVEJOY. Hey, what's going on ?
SERGEANT. What do you want to do that for ?
MRS. LOVEJOY. Now you've got to arrest me. I'll do it again if you don't.
SERGEANT (*backing*). Now then !

(*She knocks it off again.*)

MRS. LOVEJOY. There now.
SERGEANT. All right, then. I arrest you on a charge of assaulting the police and anything you say I warn you may be used in evidence against you.
MRS. LOVEJOY. Right ! (*She puts on her hat.*) Help me with that coat, Betty. The bacon for your father's breakfast's under the plate in the larder. And don't forget to ring up the *News Herald* and tell 'em what's happened. Tell 'em I've struck a blow for freedom. Come on, Sergeant, follow me !

(*She opens the door and the* SERGEANT *follows.*)

CURTAIN.

ACT III.

(*The same. Saturday afternoon one month later.* Lovejoy *stands at the sink, in shirt-sleeves, apron and bowler-hat, washing up a pile of pots. Outside someone is evidently making a speech, for we hear hand-clapping and cheers. Plate in hand he goes to the door to listen.* Joe *enters with a tray of tea-things.*)

Lovejoy. Here, what's going on out there ?
Joe. Haven't you heard ?
Lovejoy. No, what ?
Joe. They're making a presentation to mother.
Lovejoy. Who's making a presentation ?
Joe. The Northern Hikers' Association. Because she opened up the right of way on Wishton Hill.
Lovejoy. Nobody says thank you to me, and it was me sawed the notice-boards down. What have they given her ?
Joe. A silver rose bowl. And the fellow that made the presentation called mother " the flower of England's womanhood " !
Lovejoy (*sharply*). Well, why not.
Joe. Oh, all right. I've never heard you call her that, anyway. Betty says will you hurry up with them pots. There's more people want tea.

(*He empties his tray as he speaks.*)

Lovejoy. Here, wait a minute, where're you going ?
Joe. I'm going back to listen.
Lovejoy. Hey, come here and give me a hand.

(*But* Joe *has gone.* Lovejoy *scratches his head and sets to work again. The* Police Sergeant *appears at the door.*)

Sergeant. Good afternoon, Mr. Lovejoy. Busy ?
Lovejoy. Don't I look busy ? What's wrong now ?
Sergeant. Nothing. I just looked in.

(*He comes inside.*)

This blooming tea-garden of yours is giving me a lot of extra work. Headquarters'll have to send me an extra man.

(*He sits down and removes his helmet.*)

LOVEJOY. Given *you* a lot of extra work, has it ? What about me ?

SERGEANT. Regular traffic problem in the village, what with motor cars and bicycles.

LOVEJOY. Bit of work for a change'll do you chaps no harm.

SERGEANT. Now, now, Mr. Lovejoy, don't forget you owe a lot to me.

LOVEJOY. What do you mean ?

SERGEANT. Well, if it hadn't been for me, and your missus knocking off my helmet, there'd have been no case, and no scene in the police court, and you wouldn't have got no publicity at all.

LOVEJOY (*scornfully*). Publicity !

SERGEANT. There was a time when your missus would have got fourteen days without the option for assaulting a police officer. And nothing more would have been heard of the matter. But what happens ? Every paper in the country takes it up and your missus becomes a national hero. Well, don't forget it was my helmet she knocked off. What publicity do I get ? All I get's a letter from Headquarters advising me to take a course of ju-jitsu.

LOVEJOY. Ah, you was no more than a pawn in the game, same as myself. It was yon Lady Maydew she was getting at.

SERGEANT. Well, she's got at her all right. Her ladyship's left the district. Gone to live with her daughter at Cheltenham, they tell me.

LOVEJOY. What's happened to that son of hers ?

SERGEANT. They tell me he's living up at the Hall all by himself.

LOVEJOY. He's never showed up here since that night a month ago. Bit queer in the head, I reckon.

SERGEANT. Maybe you're right.

(*He surveys the pots.*)

Have you got to wash up all them pots ?

LOVEJOY. I have that.

SERGEANT (*laughing*). Well, you are domesticated and no mistake !

LOVEJOY. Domesticated ! Do you know I'm a skilled carpenter ? Look at me now. Tied to the kitchen sink. I've never had to work so hard in all my life, and all because the missus wins a bit o' brass in a football pool.

SERGEANT. I wouldn't do it.

LOVEJOY. Oh, wouldn't you ?

SERGEANT. Men should never do woman's work. It's not right. Once let 'em think you can do it and you're done for.

There's no woman in this world would get me to do work in a kitchen.

(MRS. LOVEJOY *has appeared behind him. She carries a hot-water jug in one hand and a silver rose-bowl in the other.*)

MRS. LOVEJOY. Look, George ! See what they've given me.
LOVEJOY (*taking it*). My ! That's a handsome piece.
SERGEANT. They *have* done you proud, Mrs. Lovejoy.
MRS. LOVEJOY. Hello, Sergeant ! You looking for work ? Just fill that from the kettle, will you ?

(*She gives him the hot-water jug. He obeys unwillingly.*)

LOVEJOY (*reading*). " Presented by the Northern Hikers' Association to Mrs. George Lovejoy. In recognition of her public spirit in resisting the tyranny of landlords." But what about me ? I sawed them notice-boards down.
MRS. LOVEJOY. Yes, but you didn't knock the copper's helmet off.

(*The* SERGEANT *stands with the hot-water jug in his hand.*)

Oh, Sergeant—would you take that to the lady at the table by the gate ? On the right as you go out. Thank you. Good afternoon.
SERGEANT (*grumbling*). Oh, all right. Good afternoon.

(*The* SERGEANT *goes with the hot-water.*)

MRS. LOVEJOY. Now, George, get on with them pots. No time to stand talking with policemen.

(*She picks up two plates of bread-and-butter, and goes to the door.* GERALD *appears with a roll of papers under his arm.*)

GERALD. Oh, how do you do, Mrs. Lovejoy ?
MRS. LOVEJOY. Well, if it isn't the young baronet ! Haven't seen much of you lately. How's your ma ?
GERALD. My mother's gone away, you know. She's living at Cheltenham.
MRS. LOVEJOY. Is she really ? We're very busy. Is there anything we can do for you ?
GERALD. As a matter of fact I wanted to talk to Mr. Lovejoy.
MRS. LOVEJOY. Did you ? Well, he's busy too. Sure you wouldn't like to talk to our Betty ?
GERALD. Well, to tell you the truth I would like a word with her.
MRS. LOVEJOY. Right, I'll tell her.

(MRS. LOVEJOY *smiles and goes.* GERALD *comes into the kitchen.*)

GERALD. Quite a crowd here to-day.

LOVEJOY. There is and all !

GERALD (*surveying the pots*). Gosh ! Have you got to wash all those ?

LOVEJOY. Yes.

GERALD (*removing his jacket*). Here, let me give a hand.

LOVEJOY. You ?

GERALD. Yes, me. Why not ?

LOVEJOY. Well, you can if you like. But washing-up needs a bit of skill, you know.

(LOVEJOY *juggles with a plate which drops and smashes.*)

There you are, you see. You're all putting me off.

GERALD. All right. I'll leave the washing to you, and I'll wipe.

(*He takes a cloth.* LOVEJOY *looks at him suspiciously.*)

Are these washed ? Right. (*He dries a plate.*) I'll put them on here, shall I ?

LOVEJOY. What's the matter ? Have you joined the Boy Scouts, or something ?

GERALD (*laughing*). No. But I want your advice. I think you can help me, so I'm helping you.

LOVEJOY. What do you want ?

GERALD. I'm going to turn Maydew Hall into a hotel. I've got the plans there. (*He points to the roll of papers on the table.*)

LOVEJOY. Where do I come in ?

GERALD. I believe you're a skilled carpenter.

LOVEJOY. That's right. (*They are drying the same plate as they talk passing it to and fro.*)

GERALD. There's a lot of alteration to be done, of course, and that's where you can help. You see, I'm going to employ local labour as far as possible. I've got to build in bathrooms and alter the shape of things here and there—and well, there's a lot of work for a skilled carpenter if you'll do it.

LOVEJOY. A hotel ? Do you think your mother'll let you ?

GERALD. Mother's gone to Cheltenham. She'll be much happier there. I'm boss in my own house now.

LOVEJOY. That's right, lad. You wear your own trousers. Not like me.

GERALD. From now on I'm going to turn a bankrupt estate into a paying concern.

LOVEJOY (*drying his hands*). Let's have a look at them plans.

(GERALD *spreads the plan on the table.*)

GERALD. That's the first floor. This is the second floor. All

these rooms here I'm going to divide into two. Then by running
a partition across there I make the main entrance here.

Lovejoy. What you want is a four-inch framework running
up and covering with plywood or summat o' that sort.

Gerald. That's the idea.

Lovejoy. By gum !

Gerald. What's the matter ?

Lovejoy. It's my hands. Do you know they get that hungry
for the feel of a bit of good wood, I don't know what to do ? I
could do with a job like that.

Gerald. I thought you would.

Lovejoy. Got any money ?

Gerald. I think I can raise it. The bank's been very decent.
I'm selling all the land on the far side. Then there's the timber.
Do you know anything about timber ?

Lovejoy. I know it's been neglected something cruel round
here. You want to do a lot of cutting and planting.

Gerald. We'll have to talk about that.

(Gerald *opens another plan.*)

Now here's the lay-out of the bedrooms . . .

(Mrs. Lovejoy *enters carrying a tray.*)

Mrs. Lovejoy. Now, you two, what do you think you're
doing ?

(Lovejoy *goes back to the sink.*)

Gerald. I'm afraid it's my fault. I was showing your husband
my plans for converting Maydew Hall into a hotel.

(Mrs. Lovejoy *busies herself putting teas on her tray.*)

Mrs. Lovejoy. You are going to be busy.

Gerald. Yes, it was Betty's idea originally.

Mrs. Lovejoy. Was it ? Don't let her go putting too many
ideas in your head. What does your ma say about it ?

Gerald. Well, I don't think she'll be enthusiastic. But something has to be done. Look here, Mrs. Lovejoy, I understand
you take in visitors.

Mrs. Lovejoy. We've got a room over the stable. But you'll
have to see Betty about that. She's taking charge of that side
of things. Here she is now. You'd better ask her.

(Betty *appears carrying another tray of dirty pots which she puts down
beside the sink.*)

Betty, here's your boy-friend again.

F

(BETTY *gives* GERALD *a cold greeting*.)

BETTY.   Good afternoon.

GERALD.   Good afternoon.   I was just asking if you could take me in here as a paying guest.

MRS. LOVEJOY.   He means a lodger.

BETTY.   You seem to have made yourself at home already.

LOVEJOY.   Doesn't do badly with a wiper, neither, though I wouldn't trust him with the washing yet.

(MRS. LOVEJOY *is going with a trayful of tea-things.   She turns in the doorway.*)

MRS. LOVEJOY.   Father!

LOVEJOY.   Hello?

MRS. LOVEJOY.   I want you.

LOVEJOY.   What's the matter?

MRS. LOVEJOY.   One of these tables wants fixing.

LOVEJOY.   Oh, all right.

(*He follows her.*   BETTY *has started to cut bread and butter.*)

GERALD.   You seem to be terribly busy.

BETTY.   Yes, I am.   What exactly have you come here for?

GERALD.   I came here to see your father.   Here, let me do that for you.

BETTY.   Are your hands clean?   Wash them.

(*He washes them at the tap.*   BETTY *arranges things on a tray.*)

GERALD (*as he washes*).   I wanted to see you, too.   I wanted to tell you I've done everything you said I ought to.   I'm boss of my own estate.   I'm going to turn the house into a hotel.   I'm raising money by selling land and timber.

BETTY.   And what do you want to come and live here for?

GERALD.   I'm getting a bit sick of being alone.   Do you know I've been living at the Hall for three weeks.

(*He cuts bread and butter.*)

BETTY.   Are you living there alone?

GERALD.   Yes.

BETTY.   Why?

GERALD.   I suppose—well, mainly because I've nobody to live with.

BETTY.   If you're trying to make me sorry for you it won't work.   Don't cut it so thick.

GERALD.   Will that do?

BETTY.   That's better.

GERALD. You don't seem to understand. I've done all this for *you*.

BETTY. For me? Why?

GERALD. Because I love you. I told you so that night. I was perfectly serious.

BETTY. But you haven't been near for a month.

GERALD. That's because I wanted to be able to tell you what I'd done before I saw you again. I've made all my plans—exactly as you said. In fact I'm a reformed character. There's your bread and butter.

BETTY. I want three spoons and three knives. Over there in the drawer.

(She fills a teapot.)

GERALD. These?

BETTY. That's right.

GERALD. Look here—I must have a talk with you.

BETTY. Must you?

GERALD. I want you to marry me.

BETTY. You what?

GERALD. I want you to marry me. I'm perfectly serious. I've thought it all out. I need a woman like you to help me.

BETTY. Another spoon, please.

GERALD. You see, you're just the kind of woman I want. You've got common sense and you're good at figures. . . .

(He hands her a spoon.)

BETTY. A tea-spoon not a table-spoon.

GERALD. Oh, sorry. I know I'm putting this awfully badly. I know I've said all the wrong things, but you never give me a chance to talk to you properly. Listen, Betty, I love you. Yes, I do. You're marvellous! You've got the loveliest, prettiest, sweetest face I've ever seen in my life. I've been thinking of nothing else but you for a whole month. I adore you, Betty—your eyes, your nose, your lips, your hair—everything—you're grand—you've got to listen. . . .

(She puts the tray in his hands.)

BETTY. Take that outside, please.

GERALD. You do understand me?

BETTY. Yes.

GERALD. Well, don't you love me at all?

BETTY. Hurry up with that tray, please.

GERALD. Oh, all right.

(He goes as JOE *comes in.)*

JOE (*looking after* GERALD). I say, isn't he making himself useful !

(BETTY *powders her nose at a mirror.*)

BETTY. What do you want ?
JOE. Me ? Dad sent me. He wants his 'ammer.
BETTY. His what ?
JOE. 'Ammer. What you knock nails in with.
BETTY. H—ammer !
JOE. That's what I said.
BETTY (*desperately*). Oh, it's no good.
JOE (*getting the hammer*). I don't know what's wrong with you. You do carry on queer. (*Confidentially.*) Are you in love with that chap ?
BETTY (*crossly*). Oh, go away ! You don't understand.

(MRS. LOVEJOY *comes in.*)

MRS. LOVEJOY. Joe ! Your father's waiting.
JOE. Right, ma.

(*He goes out.* MRS. LOVEJOY *takes the hot-water jug she is carrying to the fire and fills it from the kettle. Then as she goes to the door she stops to look at* BETTY *who is stabbing a piece of bread with a carving knife.*)

MRS. LOVEJOY. Don't be a fool.

(MRS. LOVEJOY *goes out, meeting* GERALD *as he comes in. She closes the door after her leaving the two together again. He shakes some coppers in his hand.*)

GERALD. What shall I do with these ? Somebody left two-pence on the table.
BETTY. You'd better keep it. It's a tip.
GERALD (*putting it in his pocket*). Gosh ! The first money I ever earned. Look here, have you thought over what I said ?
BETTY. Yes.
GERALD. You've not been crying, have you ?
BETTY. No.
GERALD. Looks rather like it. Haven't you anything to say to me ?
BETTY. Yes. Please go away and don't bother me any more. I like you very much. But can't you see that it's all wrong ?
GERALD. What ?
BETTY. You and me.
GERALD. I don't see why.
BETTY. I know I let you kiss me that night. But I didn't know you were Sir Gerald Maydew. I suppose you think that's

an attraction. Mill-girl to mansion, and all that sort of thing.
Well, it won't wash nowadays.

GERALD. Aren't you being rather old-fashioned ?

BETTY. Here, have you ever done an honest day's work in
your life ?

GERALD. Well, no, I don't suppose I have.

BETTY. Then you aren't my sort.

GERALD. I could, you know. If we start this hotel . . .

BETTY. You'd still be Sir Gerald. You can't get away from
the class you belong to.   .

GERALD. Oh, what does class matter ? I love you and that's
all I care about.

BETTY. Don't you ever believe that class doesn't matter.
Listen—my mother drops her aitches—father drinks tea out of
his saucer. How would your mother like that ?

GERALD. She needn't come to tea.

BETTY. Oh, you can laugh. You look down on our sort—
you can't get away from that. Yes, and if you'd like to know
we look down on your sort, with your nice soft ways and your
Oxford talk. Love's blind, they say, but it's not so blind as all
that.

GERALD. Betty, these are silly things—little things . . .

BETTY. It's little things that count when you're wed. Oh,
can't you see what I'm trying to save you from ? I know it's fine
being modern and all that—but these old things still matter.
You think you love me now, but you'd soon get fed up, and
you'd begin to hate my family—and you'd end by hating
me. . . .

(*She is breaking down. He takes her suddenly in his arms.*)

GERALD. Darling ! I'd never hate you . . . never in a
thousand years. Look here, you love me, don't you ? I know
it's true. Why don't you admit it ? You wouldn't care about
being hated if you didn't. You do love me, don't you, Betty ?

BETTY. Yes.

GERALD. There you are, then ! It's all right.

(*He kisses her again and again in spite of her struggles.*)

It's all right, Betty, it's all right !

(LOVEJOY *appears, hammer in hand.*)

BETTY (*struggling*). It isn't. It isn't. Please don't . . . Let
me go !

GERALD. Betty, listen to me . . .

LOVEJOY. Here ! Here ! Here ! What's going on now ?

(BETTY *breaks away.* LOVEJOY *waves his hammer at* GERALD.)

So that's what you came about, is it? Coming in here with plans, and pretending you wanted to see me, and all the time you're carrying on with my daughter.

GERALD. Betty and I thought we were alone.

LOVEJOY. I should hope you did.

BETTY. Please don't interfere, father.

LOVEJOY. But I will interfere. I reckon this is my business and I'm going to settle it. Look here, you (*to* GERALD), I've no objection to the aristocracy so long as they keep their place.

GERALD. But . . .

BETTY. Mind your own business, father.

LOVEJOY. You leave this to me, Betty. Now, you young scoundrel, what have you got to say before I give you a damned good licking?

GERALD. Only this. I've just asked your daughter to marry me. I don't think that's anything to be ashamed of.

LOVEJOY. You what?

GERALD. I asked her to marry me.

LOVEJOY. Well, I'll be . . . (*He retreats to the door and calls.*) Mother! You're wanted. Hey, Joe, tell your ma I want her. (*He comes back.*) Impudent young devil!

BETTY. He's nothing of the sort.

LOVEJOY. Oh, isn't he? So you're on his side, are you? I've heard of village squires before. He's not going to marry you. Not him.

BETTY. I know that, because I refused him.

LOVEJOY. Quite right, too.

BETTY (*truculently*). But I would if I wanted to.

LOVEJOY. No, you wouldn't. I'd have summat to say about that.

BETTY. I should please myself.

LOVEJOY. Look here, young woman, I've seen his sort before. I told you to watch your step. . . .

(MRS. LOVEJOY *comes in.*)

MRS. LOVEJOY. Now, then, what's all the trouble?

LOVEJOY. It's young baronet chap. He's been making love to our Betty.

MRS. LOVEJOY. She doesn't look much the worse for it. (*To* LOVEJOY, *in an undertone.*) I told you to keep out of here.

LOVEJOY. But he's asked her to marry him.

MRS. LOVEJOY. And what did she say?

BETTY. Oh, what do you all want to go making a public meeting of my private affairs for? I said " no " to him, of course, because we're not his kind. But he's such a fool he can't see it. You've no right to accuse him of being dishonourable. He may be a fool, but he's quite in earnest.

MRS. LOVEJOY (*to* GERALD). Don't seem to manage things very well, do you? What do you want to propose for on a busy afternoon? Have you fixed up your room?

GERALD. Well, I'd certainly like to stay here—if you'll have me after all this.

MRS. LOVEJOY. Of course we'll have you.

BETTY (*with decision*). He can't stay here.

GERALD. Of course if you'd rather I didn't . . .

MRS. LOVEJOY. Don't be soft! We aren't missing a bit of business just because Betty won't have him for a husband. (*To* GERALD). Twenty-five shillings a week all in.

GERALD. That sounds all right.

LOVEJOY. Ma—you aren't letting him live here?

MRS. LOVEJOY. Why not? (*To* GERALD.) Payable in advance.

(*She holds out her hand.*)

GERALD (*getting out his wallet*). Oh, I see.

(*He counts out the money.*)

BETTY. But we're not going to have him staying in this house.

LOVEJOY. No, it doesn't seem right, somehow.

MRS. LOVEJOY (*taking the money*). You'll have to make yourself useful. This isn't a hotel, you know. And no nonsense. Here —take this jam to the table in the far corner, and ask 'em if they'd like more bread and butter.

GERALD. Certainly.

(GERALD *takes it and goes out.*)

LOVEJOY. Here, ma, you can't treat him like that.

MRS. LOVEJOY. Why not?

LOVEJOY. Well, he *is* a baronet, you know.

MRS. LOVEJOY. I'm starting as I mean to go on.

LOVEJOY. I don't like it. Having him as a lodger. It isn't natural.

MRS. LOVEJOY. It's twenty-five shillings a week.

BETTY. Very well, then. It's my turn to speak now.

MRS. LOVEJOY. What is it?

BETTY. If he comes here, I go.

LOVEJOY. What?

MRS. LOVEJOY. Don't talk soft!

BETTY. I mean that. What's he going to think of us? Anyway, I'm not going to be in the same house with him.

LOVEJOY. Where are you going to, Betty ?

MRS. LOVEJOY. Nowhere. She's only talking.

BETTY. Yes, I am. I'm going back to my job. Father's right. It's unnatural. We don't belong here at all. We can't mix with people like that. I never want to see him again. And I shan't. He won't get the chance. Have him here if you like, if you want to make money out of him, but I'm going, and I'm going now. So there !

(*She rushes upstairs in a storm of rage and tears.*)

LOVEJOY (*scratching his head*). Ma . . .

MRS. LOVEJOY. Well ?

LOVEJOY. She's in love.

MRS. LOVEJOY. Eh, you men are so clever. It must be intuition. Didn't I see she was in love with him the first moment he set foot in this house ?

LOVEJOY. You never said owt to me.

(GERALD *returns, carrying a suit-case.*)

GERALD. I thought I might bring this in. But I want you to understand that I've no wish to stay here if I'm intruding in any way. . . .

MRS. LOVEJOY. Here, George, take this bag up to his room.

LOVEJOY. Me ?

MRS. LOVEJOY. Yes, you.

LOVEJOY. Let him take his own ruddy bag.

MRS. LOVEJOY (*threatening*). George !

GERALD. It's all right—I'll take it.

MRS. LOVEJOY. You be quiet. George ! That bag !

(*He takes it up muttering* " From skilled carpenter to blarsted lackey " *and goes out.*)

GERALD. Look here, I don't want to make a nuisance of myself.

MRS. LOVEJOY. You can't help it—sit down, I want to talk to you.

(GROCER'S GIRL *appears.*)

GIRL. Ow . . . good afternoon, Sir Gerald. I thought you'd be here. (*She giggles.*) I'm sorry about this. I took it up to the hall. There wasn't nobody there. I'm very sorry.

(*She gives* GERALD *a wire.*)

MRS. LOVEJOY. What is it ?

GERALD. It's a telegram for me.

(*He opens it.*)

GIRL (*over to* MRS. L.). It's from his mother. She's arriving on the 4.30 and she says it's got to stop.

MRS. LOVEJOY. What's got to stop?

GIRL. I don't know—I'm very sorry but it's got to stop.

MRS. LOVEJOY. Here *you*, get out!

(GIRL *exits with curtsey.*)

Impudence! Poking her nose into other people's telegrams. (*She takes it from* GERALD.) Here, what does she say?

GERALD. She's coming to see me. I think she'll be at the hall by now. You see I wrote and told her I was going to ask Betty to marry me. I'm going abroad if she won't.

MRS. LOVEJOY. Now lad, listen to me. You're in love with our Betty, aren't you?

GERALD. Good lord, yes.

MRS. LOVEJOY. All right. Then let me tell you something I've learned for myself. If there's owt you want in this world you've got to fight for it. Chance doesn't come so often, but when it does you've got to take it. I always said to myself—if ever I have a bit o' luck I'll show 'em. Look at you—all the chances and all the luck in the world.

GERALD. But it's no good if Betty won't have me.

MRS. LOVEJOY. Who says she won't have you?

GERALD. She does.

MRS. LOVEJOY. Go on. What does she know about it? No girl can think straight when she's in love. Oh, I've been watching her these last few weeks. It's a bad case, I can tell you.

GERALD. Is it really?

MRS. LOVEJOY. Aye and when I look at you it makes me wonder what all the fuss is about. She always did have queer tastes. Have you got your motor car here?

GERALD. Yes.

MRS. LOVEJOY. Right—you come with me. I've got a little plan.

(*They start to go.* LOVEJOY *meets them at the door.*)

LOVEJOY. What's going on?

MRS. LOVEJOY. You get on with them pots. (*To* GERALD.) Go on, you.

(GERALD *exits.*)

LOVEJOY. Look here, Ma, I don't like it. What'd all my pals say at home if they heard I'd got a baronet for a son-in-law.

MRS. LOVEJOY (*going*). You'll have to swallow your pride, that's all.

LOVEJOY. Well I'm against it on principle. (*Shouting after her.*) Besides I don't think he's all there.

(He returns to sink and washing up. BETTY *comes downstairs, dressed for street, looks under table, then under dresser, where she finds her shoes. She picks them up and runs upstairs again.)*

Now look here . . . Betty.

(He returns to the sink. JOE *comes in with a tray of pots, which he bangs down on table near sink. Then to centre table where he puts down some cash.)*

JOE *(as he enters).* I say, where's Betty ? I can't look after the blooming tea-garden for her. Do you know four customers have just walked out.

LOVEJOY. All right, help me with these pots.

JOE. I can't. I'm busy in the garage.

(He goes.)

LOVEJOY. Hey ! Joe, come back.

(He turns back to sink, knocks over some crocks, turns and finds LADY MAYDEW *has entered.)*

Now what the hell do you want ?

LADY MAYDEW. I want to see my son. Is he here ?

LOVEJOY. Aye, he's here all right.

LADY MAYDEW. I also want to see your daughter.

LOVEJOY. Oh you do, do you.

LADY MAYDEW. And I want to see your wife.

LOVEJOY. Have you an appointment ?

LADY MAYDEW. I received a letter from my son this morning. A very incoherent letter. He talks wildly about a girl called Betty. I presume she's your daughter.

LOVEJOY. That's right.

LADY MAYDEW. He tells me he wishes to marry her.

LOVEJOY. Well. Why not ?

LADY MAYDEW. It's unthinkable.

LOVEJOY. Why ?

LADY MAYDEW. Why—because it's impossible. After all, he is a Maydew.

LOVEJOY. Well, our Betty's a Lovejoy.

LADY MAYDEW. Now Mr. Lovejoy, there's really no need for us to be unpleasant. We must discuss it calmly. This is just a romantic infatuation and we shall have to deal firmly with these young people.

LOVEJOY. Are you going to tell me our Betty is not good enough for your Gerald ?

LADY MAYDEW. My dear man, I know nothing whatever about your Betty, but I know a great deal about my son. I know

he's a mass of queer ideas and contradictions. Look what he's
done with the estate. I did my best to save it. But I can't let
him ruin his life without doing something to prevent a dreadful
mésalliance.

Lovejoy. A what?

Lady Maydew. A mésalliance.

Lovejoy. Our Betty is not that sort of girl.

(Mrs. Lovejoy *enters* c.)

Mrs. Lovejoy. Now what's going on?

Lovejoy. Here's Lady Whatshername come for her son.

Mrs. Lovejoy. Good afternoon. This is a surprise.

Lovejoy. She's saying things about our Betty.

Mrs. Lovejoy. I know. Betty's a scheming little hussy who
trapped her poor innocent boy. It ran in *Peg's Paper* when I was
a girl.

Lady Maydew. How far has this stupid affair been allowed
to go?

Lovejoy. It went a bit too far for my liking.

Lady Maydew. Well, I shall very soon bring it to an end.
I think I can make your daughter understand.

Lovejoy. Here she is.

(Betty *comes downstairs with suitcase.*)

Mrs. Lovejoy. Come on, Betty—you're wanted. What
have you got that bag for?

Betty. I'm going.

Lovejoy. Going where?

Betty. I told you. Back to my job.

Lady Maydew. I understand this has something to do with
my son.

Betty. Yes.

Lady Maydew. Tell me, did he ask you to marry him?

Betty. Yes.

Lady Maydew. So you don't care for him, my dear.

Betty. Yes, I do.

Lady Maydew. You mean you refuse him?

Betty. You see, Lady Maydew, your lad's the sort that leaps
before he looks and I don't want him to do anything silly—
anything he'd regret afterwards.

Lady Maydew. That's extremely thoughtful of you, my dear.

Betty. He does need looking after, Lady Maydew.

Lady Maydew. Do you think so.

Betty. Well, Mother, I'm going now. Goodbye, Dad. (*She
kisses him.*) I'll stay at Aunt Sarah's until I get fixed. And I'll
come and see you week-ends. Cheer up, Dad. (*Picks up bag.*)

And don't work too hard, Ma. (*To* LADY MAYDEW.) I like your
son very much indeed. That's why I'm going . . . (*She goes.*)

LOVEJOY. Hey, Ma! Stop her! Fetch her back.

MRS. LOVEJOY. Stop her yourself. She's your daughter as
much as mine.

LOVEJOY. She's taken leave of her senses. (*Calling at window.*)
Betty. I never thought our Betty would behave that way.

MRS. LOVEJOY. Now, George. You can't talk. You didn't
behave yourself very reasonable when you were in love.

LADY MAYDEW. Anyway, she's a very sensible girl.

LOVEJOY. She is that. She's got a lot of sense has our Betty.
Even when she was a little girl, only so high, she'd come out with
sayings that'd surprise you. Do you remember, Ma?

(*He gets enthusiastic.*)

MRS. LOVEJOY. Not now, George.

LADY MAYDEW. I withdraw anything I may have said
against her.

LOVEJOY. Very well, I withdraw anything I may have said
against your lad. (*Over to* LADY M. *and offers hand.*) Put it there.
Here, Ma, what about a cup of tea?

LADY MAYDEW. I hope we shall hear nothing more of this
unfortunate business.

LOVEJOY. Aye, it's been a rum do. All the same I bet you
gave the lads a bit of trouble yourself when you was a girl. Eh?
I bet there was a bit of chase-me-Charlie in your young days . . .
(*He gives her a playful slap.*)

(*The* GROCER'S GIRL *appears with a basket of groceries.*)

MRS. LOVEJOY. Now, what's brought you here?

(*The* GIRL *giggles hysterically.*)

What's the matter?

GIRL. It was just like the pictures.

LOVEJOY. Pictures. What's wrong with the girl?

GIRL. I'm sorry—but I couldn't help seeing what went on
between him and your Betty, could I?

LADY MAYDEW. Between whom?

GIRL. Him. Sir Gerald. At the back of the garage.
Ooh, it was wonderful. . . . When she came out with her bag,
he stopped her and he said, "Where you going?" She said,
"Mind your own business," and he said, "Betty, I love you"
and she slapped his face. Oh! it was beautiful.

LADY MAYDEW. What happened then?

GIRL. Well, then he put his arms round her—Oh so lovely—
and he lifted her in his car and they drove away together.

LADY MAYDEW. Is this girl trying to tell us that my son has gone off with your daughter ?
GIRL. Yes, they've gone all right.
LADY MAYDEW. This must be stopped. Which way did they go ?
GIRL. Oh, they went down that way, your ladyship. Birmingham, I think they said.
LADY MAYDEW. Birmingham ! Of all places, Birmingham !

(*She goes out indignantly.*)

LOVEJOY. Ma, has our Betty gone off with the baronet ?
MRS. LOVEJOY. Don't fret—she'll be all right.
LOVEJOY. Aye, but what have they gone to Birmingham for ?
GIRL (*after a giggle*). I only said that to put her off. They've gone that way. Isn't love wonderful ?

(*She giggles and goes out.*)

LOVEJOY. Here. It's not all right. I've never been consulted.
MRS. LOVEJOY. No, there wasn't time. I gave that lad a bit of advice just now. That's why they've gone. I told him to.
LOVEJOY. You . . . Well, I'll be . . .
MRS. LOVEJOY (*coming to table with pen, ink and paper*). Now, George—there's a lot to do now Betty's gone. Take your backside off that chair and finish them pots . . .

(*He gets up and she sits.*)

LOVEJOY. What are you up to now ?
MRS. LOVEJOY. I'm filling in my football coupon. . . .

CURTAIN.

STAGE PLANS

ACT I

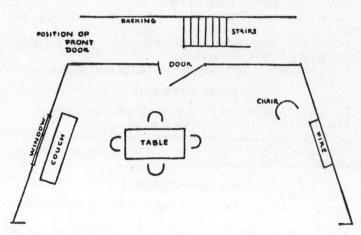

ACTS II AND III

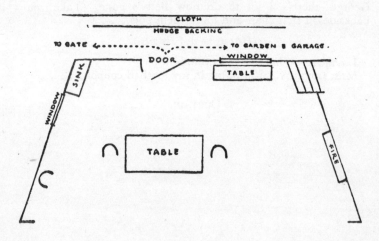

Printed in Great Britain by
Lowe and Brydone (Printers) Limited, London, N.W.10

FULL LENGTH AND ONE ACT PLAYS

A special feature of the Series is the fact that the acting fees, in addition to being moderate, are graded on a sliding scale in accordance with the nature and extent of performances. This system, which brings good plays within the financial reach of the smallest Dramatic Society, has proved very acceptable. Among the Playwrights represented are:

LIONEL HALE	AIMEE STEWART
VERNON SYLVAINE	H. F. RUBINSTEIN
R. F. DELDERFIELD	W. CHETHAM STRODE
W. A. DARLINGTON	NORMAN HOLLAND
LIONEL BROWN	PARNELL BRADBURY
TED WILLIS	T. B. MORRIS
DEREK BENFIELD	PETER COKE
L. DU GARDE PEACH	JOAN BRAMPTON
ANTHONY ARMSTRONG	ROBERT MORLEY
ARNOLD RIDLEY	NORMAN MACOWAN
L. A. G. STRONG	H. C. G. STEVENS
A. R. WHATMORE	EDWARD PERCY
RONALD GOW	WILLIAMS DINNER & MORUM
WALTER HUDD	HUGH WALPOLE
STUART READY	FRANK HARVEY
PETER BLACKMORE	BASIL THOMAS

PLAYS AND THEIR PLOTS

A Booklet giving a synopsis of the Plots, details and numbers of Cast, Scenic Requirements, Length of Performance, etc., of all Plays published by us will be sent anywhere 1/6.

FOR THE LADIES—Complete List of "all-women" plays Post Free on application

PLAYS ARE SENT OUT ON APPROVAL

Acting Fees are moderate

H. F. W. DEANE & SONS LTD.
31 MUSEUM STREET, LONDON, W.C.1

ONE ACT PLAYS

Many of the Plays published in this Series were awarded prizes in the annual Play-writing Competition organized by the Village Drama Society (now the Village Drama Section of the British Drama League). They are more particularly suited to the requirements of smaller Dramatic Societies, but at the same time many of them have been performed by larger Societies. A special feature of the Series is the fact that the acting fees, in addition to being moderate, are graded on a sliding scale in accordance with the nature and extent of performances. This system, which brings good plays within the financial reach of the smallest Dramatic Society, has proved very acceptable and contributed largely to the success of the Series. Among the contributors are: LAURENCE HOUSMAN, MARY KELLY, IDA GANDY, SUSAN RICHMOND, MARGARET CROPPER, V. E. BANNISDALE, F. AUSTIN HYDE, OLIVE POPPLEWELL, M. E. ATKINSON, PHOEBE REES, KITTY BARNE, D. C. SALAMAN, HUGH CHESTERMAN, GEORGE TAYLOR, &c.

PLAYS AND THEIR PLOTS

A Booklet giving a synopsis of the Plots, details and numbers of Cast, Scenic Requirements, Length of Performance, &c., of all Plays published by us will be sent anywhere, 1/6.

FOR THE LADIES. Complete synoptical list of all-women plays, post free on application.

PLAYS ARE SENT OUT ON APPROVAL

Acting Fees are moderate

H. F. W. DEANE & SONS LTD.
31 MUSEUM STREET, LONDON, W.C.1.